Coping With Cult Involvement:

A Handbook for Families and Friends

Second Edition

Livia Bardin, M.S.W.

American Family Foundation

American Family Foundation
P.O. Box 2265
Bonita Springs, FL 34133
aff@affcultinfoserve.com
www.culticstudies.org (formerly, www.csj.org)
www.cultinfobooks.com
www.culticstudiesreview.org

About the Author

Livia Bardin, M.S.W., is a clinical social worker and therapist, whose specialties include cult-related cases. A member of the Family Therapy Practice Academy of the Clinical Social Work Federation, she chairs AFF's Family Workshop Advisory Board and for the past four years has presented AFF-sponsored workshops for family and friends of cult members.

Cover design by David Bardin.

Second Printing, May 2002

Library of Congress Control Number: 2001097222

ISBN: 0-931337-11-9

Table of Contents

Preface

I first began working for AFF (American Family Foundation), the publisher of this book, in 1980, shortly after the organization's founding. AFF's founders wanted the organization to study the cult phenomenon scientifically in order to educate youth and the public and help families and former group members more effectively. As a result, AFF has gone through several cycles of professional study followed by the development of practical resources. Available manpower has always been too small to meet all the needs that the organization identified. Therefore, AFF has shifted its focus over the years, sometimes concentrating on educational materials, sometimes on research studies, sometimes on resources for families, and sometimes on resources for former members.

In the mid-1980s, Joan Ross and I began working on what was to become *Cults: What Parents Should Know*, because parents of a cult-involved person had virtually no practical resources to which they could turn. Many parents praised this book, which provided a general introduction to the subject and concrete suggestions concerning assessment, communication, and strategy.

Despite such praise, I always felt that more was required. Families (spouses and siblings, as well as parents) needed a book that would get into the painful nuts-and-bolts of dealing with a cult involvement and that would help them apply the theoretical notions that others and I wrote about to their unique case. Unfortunately, after the publication of *Cults: What Parents Should Know*, AFF had to focus its limited resources on helping former group members, more and more of whom were seeking our help.

For nearly 10 years, I waited for an opportunity to return AFF's focus back to families. In 1996 "opportunity knocked" when AFF volunteer professional, Livia Bardin, expressed interest in planning and conducting workshops for families concerned about a loved one's cult involvement. Mrs. Bardin conducted her first family workshop in Stony Point, New York in 1997. Subsequently, she conducted workshops in Philadelphia, Chicago, Minneapolis-St. Paul, and Seattle. She has also presented educational programs on cults to a variety of mental health professional groups, as well as the general public.

Mrs. Bardin was the right person tackling the right job at the right time. She is a diligent student of the cult phenomenon and brings to the field the practical skills of clinical social work. She also knows how to clarify and organize, to cut through the fog that confuses so many families and to illuminate for them that which is important.

Mrs. Bardin developed for these workshops a collection of forms (printed at the end of chapters that address the relevant content) designed to help families think more clearly about their UNIQUE situations. When I first saw the initial drafts of these forms, I felt great relief! At last, somebody who clearly saw what was needed was meeting that need. She realized that families needed more than words and concepts. They needed concrete tools, tools that would challenge them intellectually and emotionally, tools that would empower them to understand and do something constructive about the distressing situation for which they sought help. The forms she had developed for her workshops are these tools.

This book, which was written to explain these forms, is built on the knowledge and experience gained from years of working with families in workshops and in private consultations. This is not a "fun" book. Nor is it a book that aims to "validate" feelings of anger, hurt, helplessness, and fear, although it does that to some extent. This book is a "handbook," a tool designed to help you achieve a goal, namely, to help a loved one. As with all tools, the book requires effort to learn how to use it. It is not something that you merely "read." It is something that you use, something that you wrestle with, that you come back to again and again.

If you are willing to give the requisite time and mental exertion that this book demands, I am confident that you will find it to be extremely helpful. It may not "solve" your problem, for, as Mrs. Bardin states in the Introduction, a cult involvement is often "a situation to manage, not a problem to solve." The book will, however, make you confident that you are doing all that you realistically can to manage, if not solve, the problem that has caused you so much distress.

Michael D. Langone, Ph.D.
Executive Director, AFF
Editor, *Cultic Studies Review*
May 2002

Introduction

This is a handbook for parents, siblings, spouses and others who think that someone they love has become involved in an abusive cult or related group. Cult involvement affects not only the person directly involved, but also many others. The cult member may discard family, old friends and business colleagues, discontinue a romantic relationship, terminate a marriage, and leave behind him or her a swathe of discord and sadness that takes years to mend or may never mend entirely. The book's goals are to help you gain perspective on such situations, conduct a systematic evaluation, assess realistically what, if anything, you can or should do about it, and in general, to cope.

The book does not provide detailed background information on the cult phenomenon and presumes that you already have some familiarity with the subject. See the resource list for recommended books and other sources to consult if you are new to this subject.

Throughout this book, you will see the words "cult" and "group" used interchangeably. This is in part because there is no universally accepted definition of the kind of group you are concerned with, but also because it is more important to help a person in need than to classify a group. Whether or not the group is a "cult" matters less than whether or not specific practices and behaviors are deceptive, manipulative, coercive, or abusive, and, consequently, harmful to someone you love. Unlike a medical diagnosis, which carries with it an accumulation of research, a "diagnosis" of cult involvement provides little useful information relevant to treatment. (An essay that discusses the definitional limitations of the term "cult" can be found in the reading list: AFF, 1999, *Cults and Psychological Abuse: A Resource Guide.* This and other helpful information can also be found on the AFF Web sites: www.culticstudies.org and www.cultinfobooks.com.)

Despite the hazards of categorization, it is often a relief to name this mysterious situation. Understanding how association with particular groups can affect people so drastically helps you realize that the changes you have observed are not an isolated kind of madness. There are well-established concepts of psychological influence that explain these changes and there are practical steps you can take to respond to the situation.

Unfortunately, you have probably learned that there is little public recognition of this problem, little help available, and a great deal of controversy over what is really going on and how you should feel and act about it. Some scholars and even some religious leaders dispute the concept. It is difficult for you—an outsider—to determine that someone else's radical transformation was due to deception, manipulation, or coercion. People who have not seen this happen find it upsetting to acknowledge that human beings are so susceptible to persuasion. It is both easier and more convenient for many outside the cult scene to ascribe the difficulty to your overheated imagination or antiquated prejudice. If you are a parent, you may even have been told you just have trouble "letting go."

Until the public acknowledges and recognizes that the highly manipulative processes associated with "cults" violate autonomy, most families and friends will have to cope with cult involvement on their own.

In order to protect confidentiality and emphasize that the focus of concern ought to be practices, not specific groups, this book uses no name, so far as the author knows, of an actual cult or person, except when the author refers to identified published materials as sources. To further protect confidentiality, names are changed and where necessary, other information as well, although the experiences described are real.

If you're dealing with a case of cult involvement, you have a distressing and complex problem. When the news first breaks and you begin to realize what you're up against, your emotions will be very strong. It will be difficult to pull back and look at the situation thoughtfully. But if you yield to your emotions, you are playing the cult's game.

Powerful emotions slow your thinking and cloud your reasoning. You may feel a tremendous urge to DO SOMETHING. You may read about cases where the alert parents contacted an exit counselor, persuaded the newly-recruited cult member to spend some time with them, and, two days later, it was all over. This kind of "miracle save" can and does happen, but it's not very common. It requires lots of luck, lots of resources, and a very close relationship between family members. For many, cult involvement drags on for years—**a situation to manage, not a problem to solve**. But this does not mean the situation is hopeless, nor does it mean that families are helpless.

Coping with Cult Involvement is built around the series of forms you will find at the end of relevant chapters. Originally designed for use in consultation with a mental health professional, these forms help families in distress to pull back and get some perspective on the situation. Publishing these forms with explanations and commentary offers help to families for whom a mental health professional versed in cult problems is not readily available. You will get more out of these exercises if you work with a trained professional, but you will also get useful information and ideas by working on your own. This book grows out of six years of study and feedback from families who participated in workshops I have run for AFF. Families who have used these materials report that they helped. Hopefully, they will help you, too.

It is not necessary to read the chapters of this book in order or work on the forms in any particular order. In fact, you are likely to find information that simultaneously advances your study in more than one area.

One of the useful things you can do is have several different people fill out the forms about the member and the family. Each person will have a different perspective and it will be instructive to compare and discuss differences.

You will need to reassess from time to time, and it's always good to re-assess from the same basis. MAKE SEVERAL COPIES OF EACH FORM BEFORE YOU START FILLING ANYTHING IN. (The author holds copyright to the forms. If you have purchased this book, however, you have my permission to copy them for the uses recommended in the book.) ALWAYS KEEP A BLANK COPY OF EACH FORM SO YOU CAN MAKE MORE. And, if you are concerned about more than one person in the same group, use a separate set of forms (other than the Group Profile) for each person you are assessing. Also, use the extra-wide outside margins on every page to make notes or mark passages that are especially important for you.

Chapter One:
Coping with Cult Involvement: Overview

Surprising though it may seem, most people who leave cults simply walk away on their own. Others may be expelled from the group for unacceptable behavior or because they are ill or otherwise deemed useless.

Research indicates that a significant minority, if not a majority, of "walkaways" leave because they are disillusioned, have been severely abused, have witnessed or have been forced to participate in abuse directed toward their children or other loved ones. Others appear not to have been harmed and may leave because an opportunity opens in another direction or because they lose faith in the group's ideology and decide it is time to move on with their lives.

Tragically, some stay because they feel they have no alternative. They have no money, no job, and no friends outside the cult. If they left, where would they go? How would they find food and shelter? After years of dependency, they feel unable to function outside the familiar framework of the group.

Most people, over time, recognize when they are in a bad situation. When the situation gets bad enough, leaving is natural. The easier it is to leave the bad situation, the more likely people are to leave it.

Families who have lost loved ones to cults often feel great pressure to attempt an exit counseling (also referred to as an "intervention" associated with "thought reform consultation"). Exit counseling may be defined as "a voluntary, intensive, time-limited, contractual education process that emphasizes the respectful sharing of information" with members of cults. Exit counseling is different from "deprogramming," which today is associated with involuntary restraint of the cult member. Deprogramming involves major psychological and legal risks and is very unusual these days. I strongly recommend against deprogramming.

Although I support exit counseling, I recommend that you consider it cautiously. If you do it at the right time and in the right way, it may help. Done wrong, it could make things worse. Exit counseling requires elaborate planning. If you must deal with more than one person (e.g., because the involved person is married), the process becomes even more complex and is probably less likely to work. Nor is exit counseling likely to work if a person isn't ready to listen to the information the exit counselors want to present.

Exit counseling is expensive. Using your financial resources for exit counseling may affect your ability to carry out other important activities.

If you do eventually decide that exit counseling is appropriate to your situation, this book will increase your chance of success by helping you assess whether or not your cult member is ready for exit counseling. The book will also help you learn how to communicate and strategize more effectively. Exit counseling is important, both for helping a cult member figure out what the group is really about and for those who leave the cult on their own, but do not think that it is all there is. Exit counseling presumes that families diligently collect information, intelligently assess that information, work to change their behaviors when needed, and prepare to help the involved person after he or she leaves the group.

Basic Strategies

Four basic principles underlie the strategies that I believe are most likely to help you cope with cult involvement:

1. Increase knowledge
2. Stay connected
3. Build trust
4. Take advantage of opportunities

Increase Knowledge

To counter cult influence effectively, you need to learn. You must have a clear awareness of what has happened, both to the cult member and to you. You must learn about the cult and its leaders. And you must gain as much insight as you can into what is happening right now, with the cult member, with yourself, and with your family.

With this information you can improve your communication, assess the member's level of involvement, and recognize an opportunity when you see one. The chapters on *Understanding Cult Involvement*, *The Pre-Cult Identity Chart*, *About The Group*, *Member's Present Situation*, *Summary of Changes*, and *The Family and Its Resources* will help you organize this effort.

Remember, people change and situations change. Some changes, such as a birth or a death, are readily evident. Others are subtler and more gradual. We are often unaware of changes like these, even within ourselves. Come back to these forms once or twice a year, or after a family or cultic upheaval, to check what has changed and how it has changed.

Stay Connected

No matter how much you know, it's not very useful if you have lost touch and cannot apply it. Staying connected can be extraordinarily difficult (and is sometimes impossible). It may tax your patience, your tolerance, your ingenuity, and your pocketbook, because it is often of key importance to the cult that you get lost.

If you are lost, make every effort to get found. Material in the *Group Profile* will provide you with some of the help you need. *Understanding Cult Involvement, Communicating with Cult Members,* and *Finding A Missing Person* will help you overcome the barriers growing out of cult involvement.

Build Trust

Because cults often operate through trickery and deception, cult involvement may have strained or destroyed the trust between you and the cult member. He may have been indoctrinated to see you as the devil, or the unenlightened, or some other "undesirable" class of people. Therefore, lying to you and cheating you is OK. Because lying is unacceptable to most families, highly emotional conflicts may arise. The group may exploit such conflict to your disadvantage. You may feel anger, sadness, or any or all of a number of powerful feelings because of this. But if you are to help a cult member leave, he or she must be willing to turn to you and feel that you will help.

Your consistent, trustworthy behavior should contrast sharply with the lying, cheating, and hypocrisy that your dear one may have experienced in the group. *Understanding Cult Involvement, Communicating with Cult Members* and *Developing a Plan* expand on this theme.

Take Advantage of Opportunities

To catch a fish, you have to go where the fish are. You must have the right bait and you have to know a nibble when you get one. After you have read this book and worked through the forms, you will be better prepared to recognize an opportunity when you see one. But you still need a plan. The chapters on *The Family and Its Resources, Resources, Possibilities and Limitations,* and *Developing a Strategic Plan* will help you with this difficult job.

Some opportunities are small, but all opportunities are worthwhile. Be ready. Don't be discouraged if the response isn't as enthusiastic as you had hoped, or even if there is no response. You may not know for years—or you may never know—what the impact of your effort is. But one thing you do know. If you don't try, there will be no impact at all.

Conclusion

There is no template for coping with cult involvement. There is no "right" answer. Each case is different. Information and examples will help you to plan, but they will not give you a plan. Learn as much as you can about the situation and then apply your knowledge and expertise about yourselves, the cult member, and the situation in the most constructive way you can. Use your best judgment—and that means getting your thoughts and emotions working together, not at cross-purposes. Be patient. And don't hesitate to be creative.

Chapter Two
Changes

"Hi, folks, just wanted to let you know that I'm in the Okeefenokee Swamp for a training session with some wonderful people. Don't worry if you don't hear from me, we're pretty busy out here. I'll let you know my phone number when we get one."

A message like this, perhaps even left on the answering machine if no one is home to take the call, may prevent the police from listing your family member as a missing person, but is hardly reassuring to the family. Don't worry? When the recruit has effectively disappeared? When she hasn't said who the wonderful people are? Or what is keeping them so busy that she hasn't time to call? And why isn't there a telephone number? Don't WORRY?

Sometimes the change is gradual, especially when the cult recruit is living at home—first a day or an evening at a study session or workshop, then a weekend, then every weekend, then weekday evenings as well, until there is no time for anything else. Savings accounts may be depleted to pay for courses, contribute to the church, or invest in a marvelous get-rich-quick business.

The recruit becomes more and more unavailable for the family's routine needs and begins to pressure others. He may try to persuade a parent to contribute money or a spouse to join. The tension may increase as spouse or parent tries to accommodate escalating demands.

Then a breaking point may arrive. A spouse finds that a bank account has been emptied or a car repossessed for non-payment of the loan. Or the cult recruit is now insisting that it isn't enough for the spouse merely to tolerate his allegiance to The Master; she must actively express support by attending the meetings herself. Or a husband may come home from work one day to find both wife and children gone.

These are just a few samples of the distressing scenarios families encounter every day.

Sometimes you just see it—major and mysterious change—as when your formerly long-haired, pot-smoking son marches crisply into the house in a dark suit, countenance radiant with clean living, hair trimmed with military precision, and Bible in hand. You will see more when he denounces you as a servant of Satan and informs you that he is saved and cannot associate with the corrupted—namely, you.

Sometimes the terrifying moment of revelation comes as pure and simple shock—a sudden move to an unknown address, withdrawal from the family and its concerns, a transformation in appearance and lifestyle, perhaps an affirmation of a bizarre belief. You are stunned and alarmed and your intuition tells you something very bad has happened.

That's not the story the recruit tells. He says he has met a group of wonderful people who are devout Christians or truly serious environmentalists or really know how to develop his potential, and that he wants to be with these people and live the way they do. He acknowledges the change, but insists that it comes from within, that he has made a choice to join of his own free will, and that this is his life, and it's good for him.

Who is right? The weight of public opinion today tends to support his assertion and accept his picture of you as "controlling," or "refusing to separate," or "closed-minded." It truly can be very hard, especially for parents, to acknowledge and accept that a close family member has rejected their beliefs and values and adopted others. It is even more distressing when the manipulations of others seem to induce the change.

Many beliefs, particularly those that are religious, are deeply felt emotional convictions. They are often beyond or resistant to the reach of reason and can be neither proved nor disproved to the persons holding the belief.

Herodotus, the ancient Greek historian, tells a wonderful story illustrating the power and variety of human belief. The Emperor of Persia, to demonstrate the immense reach of his empire, summoned two men from opposite ends of his realm. One came from a land where the people buried their dead parents, the other from a land where the inhabitants ate their dead parents. The Emperor attempted first to bribe each man to adopt the custom of the other. Both steadfastly refused gigantic sums. Then he threatened them. Again, both proclaimed that they would suffer the most terrible tortures—even death—rather than perform so impious an act as to change their accustomed ritual of respect for their dead parents.

Belief still reigns. Activities that are illegal in the United States, such as marriage to more than one person at the same time, are perfectly legal in other countries. Beliefs that seem bizarre to most of us, such as the notion that our soul might once have inhabited a flea, are the norm elsewhere. Even within the United States, powerful conflicts rage continuously about beliefs. The conflict over slavery nearly tore the nation apart. Current conflicts include controversy over abortion, recognition of homosexual unions, and how to teach about the origins of the universe.

Are you objecting to a radical change simply because it's a big change? Because you personally disagree with the underlying belief? Or is there indeed a problem here? And if there is a problem, is it a cult problem? Sudden, bizarre behavior changes can result from medical causes, such as thyroid problems, brain tumors, or from the onset of serious mental illness, as well as from cult involvement.

One must address these questions carefully and painstakingly—and with the awareness that a child's casting off the family values and beliefs may be legitimate, no matter how painful. Even mature adults may suddenly make major changes in direction—leaving a successful career in law or engineering, for instance, to become a physical fitness trainer—with no undue influence at all.

Therefore, it is important to describe as specifically and objectively as you can just what has changed. You need to assess whether the changes are good, bad, or neutral for the recruit. Do the changes, after thoughtful consideration, appear to fit the recruit's own needs and personality? Or do they tend to make him dependent and docile, hamper his thinking processes, and remake him in the image of the leader?

The purpose of the SUMMARY OF CHANGES form is to help you address these questions. You will not be able to complete this form until you have largely completed the PRE-CULT IDENTITY CHART in the next chapter and learned at least enough about the group to answer the group-related questions. But you should get started right away. It will help clarify your own thinking. MAKE AN EXTRA BLANK COPY TO KEEP SO THAT IF, AFTER CONSIDERATION, YOU WANT TO MAKE CHANGES, YOU CAN DO SO NEATLY. If you don't have room to write all that you want, continue on an additional piece of paper.

The **name** requested is that of the person you are concerned about. Be sure to fill in the **date** because you will want to know later when you entered this information. Date any changes you add to your original description whenever you re-do the form. Try to recall as best you can the **date you began to observe changes.** When you focus on dates, you may find that in fact you began observing changes months before the recruit revealed his involvement in the group. Was he already involved at that time? Or did the changes predate any association with the group?

The next section documents changes in different areas. For this information to be truly useful, the changes you identify must be both specific and objectively verifiable.

For example, under **"Changes in Appearance,"** "nicer" or "sloppier" are your judgments about the recruit's appearance, not specific or objective observations. Exactly what was nicer or sloppier?

> "Switched from cutoffs to dress slacks"

or

> "Began wearing a nose ring"

gives you specific information that you can use to check against the group's norms.

> "Tired all the time"

could be your opinion, whereas

> "Attends meetings after work every evening until 1:00 a.m. and gets up at 5:00 a.m. to pray before going to work,"

is both specific and objective and saves having to defend and explain your opinion, since most people would agree that four hours of sleep are not enough.

"Changes in social and religious affiliation" refers to changes other than affiliation with the group you are concerned about. Has the person dropped her weekly bowling night with old friends? Has she left or joined a church? Has she taken up skydiving?

Changes in behavior can be:

1. New behaviors or behaviors not previously observed, such as chanting or exercising.
2. Cessation of previous behaviors, such as going to church or using foul language.
3. Significant difference in kind or degree of a usual behavior, such as many additional hours of daily praying or switching to a vegetarian diet.

Be specific in listing behavior changes. "Rude" does not describe what the recruit did that was rude.

"Refused to attend grandmother's funeral,"

or

"Yelled at mother to shut up,"

gives a much clearer picture of the conduct and the magnitude of the conduct and lets us ask, "Why?" This is a very important question, for we need to know whether or not the behavior is connected with group doctrine and practice.

"Changed diet" may mean the recruit eats more, eats less, stopped eating meat, started eating meat, or a combination of these and other changes. While you may want to sum up a number of changes and count them as one behavior change, list all the changes specifically. Diet changes are frequently part of a cult regime. Furthermore, insufficient food or insufficient nutrition can be important for asserting and maintaining cult control.

Diet can also be a serious health concern. A well-balanced vegetarian diet meets all normal nutritional needs, but a careless vegetarian diet or constant "cleansings" or "fasts" can endanger one's health.

Notice that the form asks you first to describe the behavior, then to rate it as positive, neutral or negative for the recruit and to explain your opinion. This is your judgment and it will help you a great deal to acknowledge honestly any positive changes resulting from group involvement. Not only is this important for your assessment of the overall effect of the group, it will help communications if you have something positive to say when you talk to your relative.

The form has space for three behavior changes. This is a completely arbitrary number. You may want to list more or fewer. If more, use a separate piece of paper to list changes and your opinion about them. If less, don't worry. Stop when you're finished, without embellishing or shrinking the list.

Next, there is space to list specific changes in lifestyle. There's no need to comment on these changes. Again, comparing lifestyle changes to the doctrine of the group will help you assess whether the changes result from group involvement or not.

Time spent with the group or in group activities is another way of measuring objectively just how all-encompassing the group involvement might be. If you are an active church member, volunteer fireman, or a regular bingo-player, for instance, compare your answer here with the amount of time you consider acceptable for your group activity. This is also helpful if you ever engage in a discussion with the recruit about the amount of time she is giving to the group. If it's OK for you to spend hours every day on your volunteer interests, why isn't it OK for her to do the same?

In what kinds of group activities does the person participate? This may give you important information about the group. Are the activities consistent with the person's usual interests? Although different from the person's usual activities, are they "in character" and consistent with the person you know or are they radically different from previous interests and activities? Are the activities related to the group's expressed purpose? Or are they primarily fund-raising and recruiting?

Other family members in the group helps to explain the recruit's involvement. Knowing about these relationships will be helpful in determining the member's level of involvement as well as in strategic discussions if you determine that the group is indeed harmful. For example, if the recruit has married into the group, you need to reckon with the spousal relationship as well as the membership. A member whose children are with the group may have to face the dilemma of leaving the children, at least temporarily, if she is to re-establish herself as a free person.

Financial commitment to the group may or may not be significant. Most members won't provide this information (they probably don't have it, anyway), so you will have to estimate as best you can, based on general information about the group. Again, once you have an approximate idea, compare your findings to your own and other people's financial commitments to comparable, socially accepted groups. Given his resources and his position, is the member's financial commitment significantly greater? People often worry about elderly relatives giving large sums of money away. It's true that it's their money, but is more money coming in to replace what they are giving? Are they reserving enough to meet their personal needs?

Recruitment experience asks you to describe as well as you can the history of the member's involvement, with specific attention to key points. The **date** may connect involvement with the group to a vulnerable period in the recruit's life. Stating **where** the person was recruited may also throw some light. Was he approached on campus? Was he in a strange town? How the person **first made contact with the group** can be quite important. Did he seek out the group independently (looking for a new church, for instance)? Did his boss suggest he attend a training? Or was he simply accosted on the street? These details will affect your approach to the situation.

Information about the **recruitment** process can reveal a great deal about a group's values. Was there deception, for instance, the pretense that the group's mission was working for world peace when in fact it is a religion? Was there undue pressure, such as constant accompaniment of the recruit or weekend retreats with insufficient sleep and no privacy? If the recruit concealed his involvement, was that done with the urging of the group? Was the recruit pressured to hurry his decision?

Although the moment of decision can be sudden and dramatic, legitimate major change of the sort that repudiates deeply instilled family beliefs usually follows a long and often anguished period of questioning and deliberation. The family may not know of the crisis, but friends often do. While concealment by the prospective convert, to avoid conflict or hurting the family, may well be part of a legitimate conversion, haste, pressure, and deception about the real nature of the group are often associated with induced, cultic conversions.

Use just a sentence or two to note **when and how you found out** about the change. Was the disclosure planned? Accidental? Spontaneous? Was the disclosure framed in a thoughtful, considerate fashion? Were there immediate attempts to get you to support or join the group?

Evidence of physical or sexual abuse is obviously an important indicator of the group's harmfulness and may be an important factor in developing your strategic plan. But it must be actual evidence, not your fears or concerns. If your adult daughter is involved in a sexually promiscuous group, you may worry that she will contract a sexually transmitted disease, but that is not evidence. On the other hand, patterned bruises, broken bones, or unusual soreness for which there is no reasonable explanation may be evidence, especially when the sufferer is a child.

If **you think anyone's life is in danger**, you need to be clear about **whose and why,** because you probably want to do something about it. On the other side of the coin, addressing this question straightforwardly and answering it "no" may relieve you of some unnecessary worry.

Knowledge of **techniques used to maintain loyalty and suppress doubts** is important both because it may explain some of the recruit's behavior and for your strategic planning. If, for instance, a "friend" always accompanies your sister on visits home, you may have great difficulty planning an intervention. If your son retreats into meditation or chanting when group beliefs are challenged, you need to develop a plan for surmounting that obstacle.

Other information you deem important is the place for you to add any information not requested on the form that you think should be here.

When you have completed the **SUMMARY OF CHANGES**, you should have a clear, written description of the differences between the pre-cult and in-cult person, an appraisal of whether these changes are good, bad or neutral for him, and a tentative conclusion about whether the changes are due to natural development or induced from without.

SUMMARY OF CHANGES

Name: **Date**

Your name and relationship to person described:

Date you began to observe changes:

Changes in appearance:

Changes in social and religious affiliations:

Changes in behavior:

Behavior	Positive, neutral, or negative	Why?
1.		
2.		
3.		

Change in marital status? If yes, describe:

Changes in occupation or employment (i.e., left school, lost job):

Changes in housing (location, style, others in household):

Time spent with the group or in group activities (state in hours per day or days per week):

In what kinds of group activities does the person participate?

Other family members in the group:

Name	Relationship	Previously in group, joined with member, recruited by member?

SUMMARY OF CHANGES (continued)

Financial commitment to group:

Fees and dues (approximate monthly costs) $ _____

Tapes, books, other purchases $ _____

Free labor (monthly, market value) $ _____

    Subtotal, monthly contributions: $ _____

    (monthly contributions) X (months in group) = Total Contributions: $ _____

Donations of real property (market value): $ _____

Other gifts and contributions: $ _____

Approximate total financial contributions to date: $ _____

Recruitment experience:

When recruited (Date)?   Where?

How did the person first make contact with the group?

Significant events in the recruitment process:

Length of recruitment period (Dates, then total time):

When (date) and how did you find out?

Evidence of physical or sexual abuse:

Do you think anyone's life is in danger?   If yes, whose and why?

Techniques used to maintain loyalty and suppress doubts:

Other information you deem important:

Chapter Three
Identity and Change—The Pre-cult Identity
Chart

Sam drops his computer engineering plans and takes a job at a carwash.

Isabel, a conservative young woman, starts wearing tight pants and see-through blouses and frequenting bars.

Frank, whose favorite treat used to be a trip to Ken's Steak House, becomes a vegetarian and constantly lectures everyone about the evils of eating animals.

Diffident young Tiffany joins a self-improvement group and starts door-to-door sales.

Major, drastic changes like these affect some fundamental elements of one's being, but may or may not affect other parts of a person's identity. In a cult situation, these changes are often grafted on, required by the group, and they may be causing the recruit some problems. To identify what has changed or not changed, to try to gauge the effect on the cult member of the imposed changes, to plan what is most likely to effect change in the future, spend some time learning and thinking about your loved one's "pre-cult" identity.

Identity is the collection of characteristics that make up one's personality—one's self. It starts with unchanging fundamentals, such as one's sex, place and date of birth, and ethnicity. A 20 year-old African-American female born in Seattle, Washington will be different from a 66 year-old Italo-American male from Brooklyn, for example. As we grow and experience life, our personality develops and changes. Our family dynamics, world and national events, and education, for instance, interact with our personal interests and inclinations. Our identity is an amalgam reflecting our past, our present, and our individuality.

Everyone's identity changes over time. Some changes, called developmental changes, grow out of our progress through life and are natural and inevitable. A five-year-old will be quite different when she becomes an adult. An elderly male nearing retirement is significantly different from himself in his twenties, just starting out in adulthood.

A second category of identity change occurs in response to a major event outside a person's control, often a catastrophe. The athlete who finds herself a paraplegic following an auto accident, the businessman whose store and stock are blown away by a hurricane, and families who discover that someone near and dear is entangled in a destructive cult are suddenly not the same. They will probably continue to change over a period of years as they struggle to cope, bit by bit, with drastically changed capacities and expectations. The changes ripple outward gradually, as the sufferers think through and arrive at critical decisions about the future.

Yet another kind of identity change might be called self-prompted change. These changes grow out of a person's own needs and desires. Such changes are usually gradual, though they may culminate in actions surprising to those not in the person's confidence. A person may move, changing from a Californian into a New Yorker (or vice versa). A person may suddenly terminate a longstanding relationship.

Self-prompted changes are not necessarily dramatic. After marrying, a couple may spend less time with and eventually even lose contact with unmarried friends. Nor are such changes necessarily beneficial. A woman may cope with loneliness by drinking, a little bit more each week, until she becomes an alcoholic.

Sometimes these changes are hardly noticed until some startling event brings them into prominence. Often, those closest to the person who has changed are not surprised and view the change as understandable, given the personality and circumstances involved.

If you are dealing with a case of cult involvement, you will probably see major personality changes. The cult member will most likely claim that the changes you see in him are his choice and are good for him. Evaluating the correctness of that claim is an important part of your overall assessment.

The purpose of the PRE-CULT IDENTITY CHART is to help you sort out specifically the most important characteristics of the cult member's personality before the changes that have disturbed you. This will help you pinpoint what has changed and weigh possible reasons for the change. You may also pick up some clues for your strategic plan.

There may be gaps in your knowledge and understanding of the person you are concerned about. If you don't know, leave the spaces blank and see if perhaps someone else can help you. It's a good idea to make several copies of the PRE-CULT IDENTITY CHART and ask several family members and friends to fill it in.

Be prepared for surprises, some of them unpleasant. You need information, even if it makes you unhappy. You may not have realized that John was jealous of Alex, or that he never forgave you for accidentally throwing away a prized possession, or that he was afraid to tell you about some trouble he was in. But this information has some bearing on the situation and it will almost certainly be useful in coping and planning. Anyway, if you cared more for your comfort than for your cult member, you wouldn't be reading this book.

At the center of the chart, write the name, place of birth and date of birth of the person you are concerned about. If you are concerned about more than one person, use a separate form for each person (including grandchildren born into the cult, even though they may not, strictly speaking, have a pre-cult identity).

Fill in the rest of the form in any order you like. The various entries are placed in a circle to emphasize that none is necessarily more important than any other and that all went into making your family member who he was. And, since they are part of his history, they are still part of him, suppressed though they presently may be.

Space to fill in the answers is deliberately sparse. Sort out the possibilities and focus on the highlights. If yours is a military family that moved every couple of years, for instance, it's not important to fill in every school your daughter ever attended. Was there one she especially hated or loved? List that one. If you absolutely need more space—for instance, if you're writing about someone with a string of degrees that won't fit on four lines—add extra lines. Below are detailed instructions for each part, with examples to help you as you work.

Education, Achievements. List here the most advanced level of education completed, writing the name of the school, the level achieved and the year it was achieved. If your cult member left school abruptly, start with the school he left. List the level he was on when he left and the year. If the person acquired advanced degrees, list both undergraduate and graduate degrees. If the person achieved recognition in other forms, such as fellowships, creative arts awards or athletic awards of distinction, list them here. BE SELECTIVE. Stick with the most important.

Strengths can refer to personality and temperament, such as "calm and cheerful;" talents, such as "gifted violinist;" or physical characteristics, like "healthy and energetic." This area calls for some serious thinking before you fill it in, and you might want to do some of the other sections first and return to **Strengths** later on. You may find yourself wanting to put characteristics like "sociable, outgoing," or "idealistic" in both the **Strengths** and **Weaknesses** categories. That's probably true, so you should go ahead and do it.

Occupation(s), Long-range plans refers to the person's life outside the home. Sometimes occupations differ drastically from career aspirations— for example, a young woman who wants a career in acting may be earning her living as a waitress. Sometimes people can't make up their minds and shift from job to job, so this list might come out something like, "retail sales, dental assistant, or landscape gardener." An honest, appropriate entry might be, "whatever paid the rent, no long-range plan known."

Friends have room for three. Think carefully about this and try to select at least one who has known the person a long time and one who knew him while he was being recruited into the group. One way to decide if someone was a "friend" is to think how well he or she could fill out this form (although you won't necessarily want her to do it.) If there was a romantic involvement that the cult interrupted, list that person here. Since this is a "pre-cult" chart, list cult friends only if they were friends before the cult as well.

Interests, hobbies, likes. Some people have few, some have many. Here is the place to list things done purely out of the cult member's personal inclination, including which times of year, places, holidays, and family occasions she liked best.

Dislikes is the opposite of Likes. Dislikes may range from "peanut butter" to "loud noises" to "family reunions" and "hypocrisy." Some people express their dislikes freely and you may find you need to decide which are important to list. Others don't talk about what they dislike, and you may find this is an area where you don't have much information. It's worth giving this some thought. It could be quite important down the line that you avoid something the cult member dislikes or that you recognize something about the cult that you know the member dislikes. Consider both the importance of the dislike and its intensity. An apparently trivial dislike, such as a particular perfume, for example, may be so intense that a person leaves the room if someone is wearing it.

Weaknesses encompasses vulnerabilities (e.g., lonely), character traits (e.g., impulsive), behavior problems (e.g., experimenting with drugs, in debt), or even neutral character traits (e.g., idealistic). There are separate places for noting medical or psychological problems, family conflicts, and religious or spiritual issues, so do not enter those items here.

Personal Stresses refers to situations that may have been pressing on the person at the time he or she was recruited into the group. Was there a recent divorce? Job loss? A tough decision about a relationship or career plan coming up? Had the person recently moved to a strange town? Been in an accident or major medical crisis? Endured the death of a loved one? Undertaken the care of an aged parent? Committed to quit smoking or drinking?

Prior group involvements has only three lines. Don't list things such as a nominal membership in the Boy Scouts because Mom or Dad thought it would be good for Jim, when Jim went perhaps once a month for three months and never completed any projects. Do list groups if the involvement was intensive, even though brief, and groups like the high school band, which may not self-identify as a "group." If the person you are writing about was a big-time "joiner" and constantly involved with several groups (which she's now dropped in favor of one group), note that fact and pick out two or three that seemed to have the most significance for her.

Religion, spiritual issues is the place to characterize pre-cult concerns or attitudes. Was the person an atheist? A devout Christian? What did she think about the family's religious beliefs and practices? Was this an area of major interest?

Family members refers to immediate family—parents, siblings, spouse, and children of the cult member. Close family members who died before the cult involvement should be mentioned under **Major family changes,** especially if the death took place within the past two or three years or if it was untimely or sudden.

You may want to list as **"Family members"** relatives, including grandparents, aunts, uncles, or cousins who are particularly close to the cult member. Consider unrelated persons, such as a young adult's live-in companion, who are closely involved in his or her daily life, as family members. If the cult member is an adult with his own household, his wife and children are the family members to focus on, unless there is a special relationship with a parent or sibling. The purpose of this entry is to help establish a context. There will be much more about the family in the chapter on *The Family and Its Resources*.

Major family changes, conflicts is the place to note key events in the family history. List here marriages, deaths, moves, economic changes (upward or downward), illnesses, and other major events that shaped the member's family experience.

"Conflicts" means ongoing issues within the family, whether over specific issues or generated by contrasting temperaments. If Andrea wanted to be a musician, but her father insisted she enter dental school, that's a conflict. If Andrea's brother was the one who was pressured into a career he did not care for, that too is a family conflict. (For assessment purposes, it doesn't matter much who was right and who was wrong, but it's important that the conflict be acknowledged.) If two brothers, one naturally neat and one naturally sloppy, share a room, that's a conflict. Family secrets, such as a family member's past incarceration, cause conflict, as those not in on the secret notice mysterious behavior and wonder what it is about. Unacknowledged problems, like alcoholism, are sources of conflict.

Strive for accuracy as you think about this. Conflict flares up in all families at least occasionally and the existence of conflict merely confirms that yours is indeed a typical family.

A cult may sometimes use even family conflicts to strengthen its hold on your family member. Encouraging the cult member to form a distorted view of the family, for example, is an important recruiting and retaining gimmick in cults.

You can counter the power of this tactic if you recognize the family conflicts that are exploited by the group. Keep in mind, however, that family conflict or other family problems are not necessarily related to your loved one's cult involvement. For present purposes, it's enough to identify the conflict.

History: developmental, medical, psychological refers to the cult member's personal experience. As always, keep to the major events. It is not necessary to list an infant tendency to strep throat, or that Sandy was sad when her grandmother died. List major problems, or abnormalities that required diagnosis and treatment, both chronic conditions like allergies and one-time events like an episode of major depression. You may be able simply to write, "Normal" on the top line and go on.

Feel free to review this form once you've filled it out, to change or erase or add, and to compare and discuss your assessment with that of others.

This is the baseline you will use to measure the changes you've observed. You can then decide whether they're natural or believable developments of the person's core identity, whether they are positive, neutral, or negative in meeting the person's needs and promoting his growth and development, and whether and to what extent they reflect the needs and demands of the group and its leaders without regard to the individual.

PRE-CULT IDENTITY CHART

Date: _____

Strengths

Educational Achievements

Occupation (s)
Long range plans

Friends

Interests,
hobbies, likes

Dislikes

Weaknesses

Name:
Date of Birth:
Place of Birth:

History: developmental
medical,psychological

Major family
changes, conflicts

Family members

Religion,
spiritual issues

Prior group
involvements

Personal
Stresses

Chapter Four:
About The Group

It's almost instinctive—and a good move, too—to investigate the group you suspect is responsible for the troubling behaviors and personality changes that you've observed in the recruit. As a caring relative or friend, you want to know whether or not this is a reputable group and how its leaders are qualified and selected. You need to learn what the group believes and practices. How does the group recruit and retain members? Does it pursue its stated objectives or is it really just a power trip for the leaders?

It may be very difficult to study the group objectively. The group's machinations may have caused you to suffer severely from the alienation and disdain of a person you love. The group's practices and beliefs may be repulsive in and of themselves. The group may be teaching that you—parents, spouses, siblings or close friends of the recruit—are "agents of Satan" or "limited persons" and that association with you is detrimental or even dangerous.

Despite the understandable anger and anguish all this may cause, it is essential to learn about the group and its teachings if you are to understand what has happened and to make solid strategic decisions. Remember, if this is a destructive cult, calm, rational behavior, objective information, and clear thinking are exactly the opposite of what the group wants from you, your family, and its own members.

You cannot develop a strategy unless you know what the group professes to believe, what it does, how it might react to things you might do, whether there seems to be any immediate danger to anyone, and what your loved one might find satisfying, appealing, dissatisfying, or distasteful. You also must consider the possibility that even though the group's beliefs and practices are alien to you, it may not be destructive or deceptive. The recruit's conversion might be a perfectly legitimate change of heart and direction, or could reflect psychological problems that have nothing to do with the group.

Some groups receive a great deal of publicity because of their bizarre behavior or because they seek publicity for recruitment purposes. Some have been around for a while and accumulated a history. Others are far less conspicuous. It can be very difficult to find any objective information about a small, recently formed local group. Some of the larger groups with numerous local branches may differ significantly from branch to branch, despite a common central authority. Nevertheless, many groups will have some sort of record, however sketchy.

The GROUP PROFILE asks you to outline information that will help you assess the situation, develop a strategy, and communicate with the cult member. You may not be able to find all the information requested. In that case, you will at least be aware of what you don't know. Or you may learn a great deal more than the basics outlined in the *Profile*. The more you know, the better off you are.

Groups change. A group that began as an end-of-the-world group, stockpiling against major civil disaster, changed into a "moving-to-a-higher-level" group that engaged in mass suicide. Don't assume that things are the same now as they were two years ago. Don't assume that things will continue as they now are. Keep in touch with developments. BEFORE YOU START FILLING IN THE BLANKS, MAKE A COPY OF THE *GROUP PROFILE* so that you always have another blank to work from. **Date your work**, so you know when you entered the information. Note the sources of your information very specifically so that if you need to, you can find the documentation to support your information.

The GROUP PROFILE starts off with an introductory paragraph about the name, location, and size of the group. This may not be as simple as it sounds, since many groups have more than one name and groups often misrepresent their size. Groups may change their names as their themes change. Many move from place to place.

The best source for current information is likely to be the group itself, through its official publicity, and the member. In the early stages following revelation of cult involvement, the new member may try to recruit you, his relative or friend. After all, you should be saved or enlightened too! If the opportunity arises, take the material she presses on you, listen for the names of places she's recently been to, and ask her how many people attend the meetings.

If you can, attend a meeting or two. Network a little. Introduce yourself, "I'm Jean's mother" or "husband" or "friend," and find out something about other people there—where they come from, where they work, how long they've been coming.

Resist the pressures that are seducing Jean by noticing and mentally cataloguing which ones you can identify. Is the room pulsing with strobe lights? What kind of sound system is in use? If there's a public address system, who controls it? How long does the meeting go without a break? What happens when you get up to leave the room for a break? How long is it from start to finish? What feeling do you get from the decor? How is music used? Are there refreshments? Are you pressured to contribute money? To speak affirmatively about the group? What is the group's ritual? What is the dress code? What message does it convey?

Meetings open to you may be different from meetings for initiates, so don't assume all meetings are alike. Don't be surprised by "love-bombing." Total strangers may walk up and give you a close hug. View warm welcomes and flattering remarks as probable elements of a sales pitch.

You may find the meeting very long and boring. You may see some things that shock you, like public confessions or humiliation of members who express doubt or fail to meet quotas. Keep calm. Remember what upset you. You may be able to use the recollections in later conversations with the recruit. But don't let it be the first remark out of your mouth when she says, "Well, wasn't it wonderful?" (A possibly appropriate answer might be: "I can see why you're so enthusiastic—but it's so different. I need to go home and think about this.")

Some people, especially from families accustomed to frank and open sharing of thoughts and feelings, may be uncomfortable about holding back their reactions and observations. This is one of numerous dilemmas you will face as you work your way through the complex, difficult situation. Is it better to express your negative opinions immediately or to reserve them until they are more likely to have some weight? Remember, your short-term goal is to learn more about the group. And, should you decide it is a destructive group, your long-term goal is to extricate the member. What will work best for you and your family and the group member?

Nothing in this book is a prescription. If you find these suggested responses inappropriate, think of some other responses that will meet your needs, and that you are more comfortable about using. (Be sure to read the chapters on *Understanding Cult Involvement* and *Communicating with Cult Members* before you make a decision about this.)

Prepare some non-committal answers to likely approaches from the group. If you are singled out and asked why you're there, you can answer quite truthfully something like, "Jean has told me so much about you, and I wanted to see for myself."

You may find yourself pressured with questions such as "What do you think of us?" or observations such as "I can see you're ready to see the light."

Answer calmly: "I'm not jumping to any conclusions. I want to learn more before I have an opinion."

If you feel yourself getting drawn into the action, whether in debate, or in anger, or—yes, it happens—in agreement or sympathy, take a break. Leave the room for a few minutes. Some groups will pressure you to stay, but of course it is against the law to detain you against your will. Stay calm, but don't be afraid to assert yourself if someone tries to keep you in the room when you are ready to leave.

Some groups will try to get you to sign a release beforehand, stating that you won't sue them because of anything that happens during the session. This is an interesting signal that there has been trouble in the past or that the group is aware of some risk attached to their proceedings.

Whether or not you sign such a release, or whether or not you honor it later, is a matter for you to decide. You may just want to walk away with an unsigned copy of the release and think about it, or consult an attorney. You may want to sign it, marking it "with reservations." In fact, you're probably not going to end up suing the group for anything that happens during the session, and your objection may be the emotional one of not wanting to let "the enemy" push you around.

The group may have materials for sale—tapes, books, newsletters and bulletins, charms, foods. Buy some of the tapes and publications. They may have useful information, such as names of key staff, notices of upcoming events, the formal or corporate name of the group, the state where it was incorporated, and so forth.

It would be interesting to know who gets the money that the members hand in. If you pay by check (not credit card, as you don't want to surrender your credit card information to people who might not be honest about using it), your canceled check will tell you where the group banks and the account number. Conversely, of course, the group learns the same things about you. If you are concerned about your privacy, pay cash.

You may also be able to get an official biography of the leader through the group. This is useful because there will probably be important facts (as well as important omissions). What was the leader's birth name? When and where was he born? Who were his parents? Has he any brothers and sisters? Where did he go to school? What did he study? Did he graduate from high school? College? What is his professional or vocational training? His work history?

You can check much of this information in public records. The same information about other key leaders may be available, as well. Remember as much as you can of what people say about the leaders—their history, qualifications, personalities, and families. If you can, check the truthfulness and completeness of this information. You may begin to get a sense of the leader's character and intentions right here.

Former members are invaluable sources of information about the group. If you can, track down people named in news articles or people otherwise identified as knowing about the group. If possible, attend regional or national conferences sponsored by cult education groups. These meetings attract people from a broad geographic range and you may be able to connect with someone who had an involvement with the group.

Check the Internet for both pro- and anti- group Web sites. An increasingly large body of information is available, but remember that there is no guarantee as to its accuracy. AFF (American Family Foundation), a reputable cult education organization, maintains a site at www.culticstudies.org, with links to many other pages, both pro and con, about controversial groups. Be sure to jot down the source of any information you collect from the Internet, so that you can find it again if you need to. Make a hard copy of any information you may want to refer to again, as material may be removed between visits to a given site.

You may find it useful to consult some books about investigative techniques and strategies. One useful publication is *Investigator's Guide to Sources of Information*, published by the U.S. Office of Special Investigations, General Accounting Office (1997). You can order this free from GAO at 202-512-6000 (Stock #OSI-97-2). The text of this manual is also available online at the GAO web site (*www.gao.gov*).

Another useful publication is *How to Investigate Destructive Cults and Underground Groups*, by Zilliox and Kahaner (see Appendix B).

If the group is a large, high profile operation, you may find that a great deal of the work has been done for you. There may be books or magazine articles that detail both the leader's claims and the facts. Start at your local public library. Find the reference librarian and tell him the name or names of the group and its leader. He will also show you how to search print and electronic databases and find the publications you need.

Most cults are small, but even very small groups may have come to the attention of the local newspaper, so be sure the librarian checks those sources or tells you how to do it for yourself. If the group is headquartered in a distant place, call that city's public library. If your son was recruited from a college campus, check the local newspapers, including campus newspapers that cover the college area.

If a college or university is in the picture, check with the administration, student affairs, chaplain, or whatever department is appropriate to learn whether or not the group was allowed to operate on campus. If yes, find out what the college knows about the group's structure, finances, and leadership. If no, find out in what way the group failed to meet the guidelines for approval, or whether it failed to apply.

A group's official publications and documents will almost certainly be self-serving and may be incomplete, evasive, or outright false. Press stories tend to stress the sensational and may be superficial or inaccurate because they were produced under pressure to be timely, sensational, "even-handed," or to highlight a local personality. Information that just doesn't happen to surface in the face of a hurried investigation may be completely overlooked. Minor inaccuracies may distort the overall impact of a story. Something that would strongly affect the person you are concerned about might have been completely passed over because it was not relevant to the story. A story about fraudulent bankruptcy, for instance, might not mention that the leader pressures pregnant members to have abortions. You should check some basic sources for yourself.

At least three separate court systems operate in this country. Federal (U.S. District), state and local, and U.S. bankruptcy courts all have records that are available to the public upon request. The federal U.S. District courts will have records of any federal criminal convictions, federal tax liens, and litigation at the federal level. State courts (often called county courts) will have records about state criminal convictions, state tax liens, divorces, and state-level civil litigation. The county courts will have records of real estate transactions, credit foreclosures, and repossessions. (There may also be a separate municipal court with records of local criminal convictions and civil litigation.) All bankruptcy activity is handled through a separate set of federal bankruptcy courts.

Find which courts have jurisdiction over the group's location (The public library or local telephone books can help you with this.) Go to the clerk's office in the appropriate courthouse and ask how to access the records for information about civil litigation, divorces, criminal and bankruptcy proceedings, tax liens, real estate transactions, credit foreclosures, and repossessions. Search both in the name of the group and in the names of its leaders.

Each state also has one or more offices where marriages are recorded. In some states, drivers' records are also available to the public. If they are, get the leader's driving record. While you're at it, check your recruit's record. Has she been letting the group exploit her credit? Has she transferred property to them? Does she have criminal charges pending?

If the records show that the group owns property, check out the property. Who uses it? For what purposes? Find out from the local police if there have been any complaints about activities at that address. What kinds of complaints? Who complained?

If the group is formally incorporated, it will have *Articles of Incorporation* and some form of annual report on file and available to the public in the state where it is incorporated. These *Articles* will state the name and purpose of the group (which may be surprisingly different from its current statement of purpose), and the names and addresses of its founding officers and directors. This will tell you who the originators were. Are they still around? Are they still in the leadership circles? What has changed?

If the group is incorporated as a non-profit group other than a church, it is required to file a form with the Internal Revenue Service (IRS) every year, called Form 990. Form 990 describes the group's sources of income and lists the names and salaries of high-salaried officials.

Form 990 is theoretically available to the public, but until recently, was difficult to get hold of. Non-profit groups are required to make a copy available at their headquarters to anyone who asks for it, but this is not a very tactful way of getting it. You can also request a copy from the IRS.

You must first find the group's taxpayer identification number (provided from an index that the IRS has available in various regional offices), then write to the IRS. Some records are misfiled or lost and seldom does the IRS feel obliged to put a lot of energy into providing the information, so it may be quite a while before your request is answered, if it is answered at all.

In 1996, Congress passed legislation that requires non-profit corporations to provide a copy of the 990 by mail to anyone who writes to the organization. So if you have a friend who will help you out, you can try to get the 990 that way. Two web sites you might find helpful are: www.guidestar.org and www.nccs.urban.org/990/. The latter site claims to be able to retrieve Form 990s if you have the organization's name and state.

Churches do not have to file a Form 990. If the recruit's group has incorporated calling itself a "church" (and that's all it has to do to qualify), it may not have a 990. But check it out. Some churches don't know this and file a 990 anyway.

If the group is headquartered far from where you live, you may want to travel to the relevant county seat or state capital. Perhaps a friend or relative living in the area could help you.

You may prefer to hire a private investigator to get this information for you, or if you have lost contact, to help you find your missing family member. Investigators have ready access to major databases and they know the procedures for finding information not on these databases. They often have personal connections to other sources.

Be sure you are working with a licensed private investigator whose training and qualifications meet your needs and who has an ethical professional history. Many investigators are former law-enforcement officers, but unfortunately that is not an automatic guarantee either of competence or of character.

Most investigators charge by the hour and will be able to tell you roughly how many hours their search is likely to take, based on your description of the problem. You can control your cost by restricting the numbers of hours you authorize. Another approach is to use an investigator who will access a particular set of databases for a set fee. Appendix A has more detailed information about selecting a private investigator.

A few hours of a professional investigator's services may be a big help in focusing your investigation. If the investigator, for instance, can tell you there is no information about the group or its leaders in the federal district court or bankruptcy system, you've saved yourself some time and energy. If there is information about a state criminal conviction, the investigator can tell you how to locate more details.

As you collect information, use the GROUP PROFILE to organize it. The GROUP PROFILE is arranged in narrative form. The first paragraph, Items (1) through (4), asks for basic introductory information about the group. The next paragraph, items (5) through (12), covers biographical information about the leader or leaders. Items (13) through (18) provide space for information about the group's or leader's involvement with the law. Item (19) is for information about the group's finances. Item (20) offers space for listing members' achievements. Are movie stars members of the group? Best-selling authors? (And, by the way, is there special treatment for celebrity members?)

Space to talk about the public perception of the group (or lack of public perception of the group) is available in items (21) and (22). This is useful, as it will affect your approach to the members, and theirs to you. A group whose leader has just been convicted of income tax evasion will be somewhat more defensive than a group whose leader has just been to dinner at the White House.

The rest of the GROUP PROFILE addresses the professed ideology and activities of the group, including some examples of the group language. Finally, there is a catchall place for information that didn't fit anywhere else.

When you get the facts about the group and its leaders, compare them with the group's public representations on these topics, both factual and ideological. Is the history consistent with the group's proclaimed ideology? If there are discrepancies, are they significant? A group leader who states that he was born in Maine, but was actually born in Texas probably has a reason for lying. It could be quite significant, but it also could be inconsequential. You may find contradictions. For example, a group that claims to teach benevolence to all, but has a record of being evicted for non-payment of its rent, argues a definite lack of benevolence to landlords.

If the principal activity is fund-raising, this may cause you to suspect that the group's ideals are less important than financing its leaders. If the group's main ideological premise is that they have the one true interpretation of the Bible and that others, who do not, are lesser human beings, they may be using this stance to justify cheating, lying, or otherwise mistreating non-members.

Your investigation may confirm that the group's representations are true. In that case you must at least acknowledge their honesty (though some of their ideology or practices may still appall you).

Use the information you collect about the group's ideas, practices, and operations to begin assessing its potential for abusiveness and destructiveness, as well as the possibility that undue influence or deceptive recruiting practices were used on your family member. Look at your entries for Item (26), techniques the group uses to maintain and reinforce control. Does your list include sleep or food deprivation, isolation from family and former friends, constant accompaniment by another group member, excessive and prolonged use of thought-stopping and reinforcement devices like chanting, tapes, meditation? These practices are a strong indication that the group is using psychologically manipulative techniques.

Finally, Item (30) asks you to list and define five key words from the group's language. As you identify and study these words, remember that it's natural for all groups with a common interest to develop their own jargon. Most Americans know enough about baseball to be aware that "home plate" is not a piece of china, a "strike" does not hit anything, a "foul" is neither evil nor ill-smelling, and so on.

Group jargon exists in all groups, including the family. An outsider hearing one family member say to another, "I left my Snodgrass in the back-back," might think the person was talking about a botanical specimen forgotten in Australia. In fact, the person is saying in family jargon that he left his hat in the trunk of the car.

The issue is not that a private language exists. The importance of the group jargon lies in the actual words used, their implications, and the confusion of metaphor with reality that triggers alarm. For example, let's look at the private language of the Heaven's Gate group, which ended in a mass suicide in San Diego in March 1997.

A Heaven's Gate initiate was trained to refer to his or her body as "this vehicle." Sexual desire was labeled "addiction" and it was an important goal of "the class," as the group called itself, to "get control of the vehicle" by "re-programming," their code word for, among other things, castration.

Repeatedly referring to one's body as a machine, like "this vehicle," infers that the body can be handled and treated like a machine—if need be, taken apart and re-assembled along different lines. In the end, the group viewed suicide as a "procedure" that would enable them to get out of their "containers" and "advance beyond human."

The tragic example of the Heaven's Gate suicides horrifically illustrates a core characteristic of destructive cults. Their language is not mere metaphor. It expresses and supports the group's ideology.

Another private use of language may be the adoption of a new name. Heaven's Gate members took new names after joining the group. The new names each had a brief prefix followed by "doti" or "odi," reflecting the two leaders' appellations of "Do" and "Ti."

Knowledge of "groupspeak" is also a good test of the success of your research. If you can list five key words from the group's language and use them in a sentence the way the group would, you are demonstrating good basic knowledge of the group.

Groups, like any other living organism, don't stand still. They grow, shrink, and change. Unhappily, groups that seem fairly harmless can become lethal. The classic example is the People's Temple, which began as an idealistic group promoting racial integration and mutual support. It ended with a suicide-massacre in the jungles of Guyana in 1978 that killed over 900 people.

Sometimes groups splinter or disintegrate. A period of turmoil may offer opportunities, if you only know about it. A new leader may emerge or the old leader may have a new revelation and introduce radically different ideology or practices. Old group language will vanish and new terms and techniques will be introduced. You need to stay abreast of changes as you wait and watch for your opportunities.

GROUP PROFILE

(1) The name of the group is _____. (2) The group's

headquarters is in _____. (3) Other major centers of group

activity are _____

(4) The group has approximately _____ members (though they publicly claim _____

members).

(5) The leader's name is (or leaders' names are) _____

_____. *For each leader or key figure*: (6) His (or her) birth or

former name is _____ _____. (7) He (she) was born in _____

_____ on _____. (8) He (she) attended the following

schools:_____ _____ and

has the following vocational or professional training: _____

_____

(9) In *(year)*____, he (she) married _____, whose occupation is

_____. (10) They have _____ children, whose names and ages are _____

_____ (*If more than one*

marriage, add information about the termination of the marriage and list name and occupations

of subsequent spouses and any children of those marriages.) (11) He (she) previously worked as

(list occupation, employer, place and approximate dates if known):_____

_____

_____

(12) Experiences that mark his (her) development into a cult leader are:

_____

_____

_____

Federal, state and other court and public records show the following (13-17):

(13) Civil litigation and outcomes: _____

_____

(14) Criminal cases and outcomes:

_____

_____

(15) Tax liens, real estate transactions, credit foreclosures and repossessions: _____

_____

(16) Bankruptcy _____

(17) Driver's license and driving record _____

_____

(18) The group is also known as _____

(19) It was originally incorporated in *(year)* _____ as a *(business, church, etc.)*_____

_____ in the state of _____ *(If not formally organized, note that.).*

(20) Changes in name, purpose, location and key leaders since then include:

_____

_____

_____

(21) The names of current officers and board members are: _____

_____

_____

(22) The basic ideological premise of the group is _____

_____

(23) Members' principal group-related activities are _____

_____

(24) The group's income is about $_____ per year. The main source of income is

_____. Other sources are _____

_____

(25) Group members have been credited with the following achievements:

_____

_____

(26) Group members have been convicted of the following offenses:

_____

_____

(27) Members live _____

_____

(28) Techniques the group uses to maintain and reinforce control are _____

_____

_____

_____

_____

(29) Group beliefs and practices relating to diet: _____

(30) Group beliefs and practices relating to dress: _____

_____

(31) Group beliefs and practices relating to sex: _____

_____

(32) Five key words from the group's language are:

      Word   Group meaning

1. _____   _____

2. _____   _____

3. _____   _____

4. _____   _____

5. _____   _____

(33) The principal books, articles, and television coverage on the group are (list title, author or

show and date):

1. _____

2. _____

3. _____

(34) In general, the press seems to view the group as _____

     Add any other important or useful information about the group that is not stated

elsewhere in this profile:

Chapter Five:
Where Do Things Stand?

After carefully studying the group, and learning as much as you can about the changes that alarmed you, you are ready to decide whether:

- Despite the group's bizarre beliefs and unusual activities, you have found nothing deceptive, dishonest, or destructive about them. You can see that your loved one's affiliation, while not what you would choose for yourself or anyone else, was not stimulated by trickery or undue influence. Even though you think it is a mistake and would like to see the attachment dissolved, this is not a case of cult involvement.

Or

- You may now reasonably conclude that a valuable, beloved person has been ensnared and deluded by an unscrupulous group that is using her without regard to her own needs and interests to feed the ambitions and desires of its leadership. Yours is a case of cult involvement.

Or

- The group you are concerned about lies somewhere between the two extremes of the influence continuum. It may endanger its members through some hazardous beliefs, such as quirky ideas about diet, or engage in mildly manipulative practices, such as magical thinking about the power of mind over matter. But it does not subject its members to a thought reform program and does not exploit them in the interests of the group's leaders.

This book is primarily focused on helping people who are dealing with cult involvement and will be less useful to those in other situations. However, the chapters on *"Communicating with Cult Members"* and *"The Family and Its Resources"* might help you gain some useful insights if there has been conflict in the family as a consequence of a family member's affiliation with a less destructive group.

If this is a cult case, the next step is to make an informed appraisal about where the cult member now stands. There are two parts to this assessment: her present level of involvement with the group and intrinsic factors, unrelated to the cult's manipulations, that might affect her inclination to stay or to leave.

Determining the member's current level, or stage, of involvement is difficult because you have so little access to her inner thoughts and so much of what she says and does may be deceptive. Moreover, sorting cult involvement into "stages" suggests a kind of distinctness that usually oversimplifies the actual situation. People may go back and forth from one stage to another or may be partly in one stage and partly in another at the same time. Like all else about dealing with people, there is no formula, no simple set of directions that works. Nevertheless, the more you know about a cult member's level of involvement, the better you will be able to plan. The discussion of each stage includes comments about strategic planning considerations.

Let's talk about six different stages of involvement:

- Fringe member
- Recruit
- Honeymooner
- Veteran
- Habituated member
- Castaway

The Fringe Member

People at the fringe stage are those who participate in a limited way. For example, a person may take courses on and off, without becoming further entangled with a group. Attendance doesn't escalate to the exclusion of other interests. Involvement does not affect job performance or family relations. The financial commitment continues to be affordable. Or a person may enthusiastically sign up and initially lay out money, but his enthusiasm quickly fades as the group's demands begin to impact on other interests and activities.

Fringe involvement is not unusual, especially in self-improvement, "realize-your-potential," or multi-level marketing groups. Although you may disapprove and may have evidence that the group's practices are not necessarily efficacious or that a comparable program is available at a lower price, it would be difficult to characterize this situation as "harmful," since you are unlikely to note any adverse effects. However, since the person may deepen his involvement over time, some action may be appropriate to forestall possible future harm.

If you are uncomfortable about a person's affiliation with a questionable group, take a "watch and wait" attitude. Groups may be very harmful to some individuals, but not to others. Groups may be harmful to those who engage intensely with them, but not to those who are marginally involved. Keep yourself informed about the group and the member's level of activity, but until you have reason to believe otherwise, classify the activity as "waste of time," not "waste of person."

The Recruit

As a recruit, a prospective member is heavily involved with the group and is clearly attracted, perhaps even converted, but has not broken ties with her regular life and may still be open to questions about the group's claims. This person may listen to your questions and may even be willing to talk to an expert on the group, provided you are knowledgeable, tactful, and lucky.

If you detect the problem at this stage, you still have a chance to nip it in the bud. Be mindful, however, that it is unusual for friends and family to be let in on a recruit's involvement until after the recruit is securely *in*. Family members may think the involvement is recent because they have only recently found out about it. Think carefully about exactly when you first heard about some great new people in the prospect's life, or when you first noticed odd or secretive behavior. This frequently pre-dates any actual mention of involvement with the group, often by months.

Here's an example of prompt, successful action at the recruitment stage. You can see from this story how difficult it is, as well as the necessary ingredients for success:

> A young woman, Kelly, was spending the summer in a city far from her hometown. She was temporarily sharing an apartment with two others, one of them the son of a family friend. Kelly was very close to her parents and they often spoke by telephone. She happened to mention to her mother that she had met some interesting people and was going to spend a weekend with them at their retreat in country.
>
> The mother happened to mention this to an acquaintance who recognized both the name of the town and a well-known cult's recruitment approach. The acquaintance cautioned the mother, who laughed off the notion that her daughter was dumb enough to be fooled by the cult. Two weeks later, the acquaintance received a frantic phone call from the mother. Kelly had called to say she was leaving the following weekend for a year's

commitment with these "interesting people" and would be working to improve the lot of the poor.

Because of the conversation with her acquaintance, the mother immediately realized what was going on and lost no time getting in touch with appropriate experts. Both parents took part in a hastily organized briefing about cults in general and this well-known group in particular. Because Kelly was staying with a friend's son, the mother was able to get information to the roommates about what was happening and to get their cooperation and input.

The parents got on the next plane for the distant city, each with a book. En route, one parent read *Combating Cult Mind Control*, absorbing the basics. The other read the story of a young man who had left the group in question, including a detailed account of the recruiting process.

Arriving on the very day their daughter was scheduled to leave, the parents engaged her in a respectful discussion that questioned the group's practices, not asking Kelly to change her mind, but asking her to get answers to certain questions before leaving—in effect, convincing her that the group was controversial and she should hear the other side.

Not only was Kelly young and still dependent on her parents, they were able to point out the many ventures they'd supported her in and the total trust they had accorded her. Never before, they pleaded, had they questioned her decisions. They plainly said (and she knew they would keep their word) that if she had heard both sides, they would respect her decision, whatever it was. She agreed to listen.

Fortunately, a very capable expert was available nearby, and within a couple of days Kelly decided not to go for the year's commitment. Within a few weeks she had disengaged completely from the group.

Kelly and her parents had a very close relationship. The parents knew exactly when her involvement began and knew that she had previously spent a weekend at the group's retreat. Remarkably, she disclosed her plans in advance (evidence of her comfort level with her parents, as well as suggesting some ambivalence).

The parents had an immediate source of information and immediate support from Kelly's roommates. They were able immediately to tap into cult education resources. They were fast learners, good listeners, and gentle people who could maintain their patience and contain their anxiety so that they reduced, rather than escalated the tension.

The Honeymooner

Much can happen during the recruitment stage—but only if it really is still the recruitment stage. The next stage, the honeymoon, is the period when the recruit, now a full member of the cult, is *least* likely to respond to outside efforts of any sort. He is initiated and indoctrinated. He is in a daze of idealism and enthusiasm and sees and knows nothing but good about the group. Everyone is still wonderful to him. Everything about the group is positive and anyone who questions it in any way is negative.

Not surprisingly, this is the stage when friends and family are most likely to learn that there is cult involvement, although the full degree of commitment still may not be evident. There are good reasons for the new cult member to abandon secrecy at this point. At the practical level, she may be making radical changes, like quitting school or job, moving away, adopting a new diet or dress, that simply can't be concealed. At the personal level, the new member wants to proclaim the marvelous revelation that has transformed her, and probably also to "save" those she loves most.

From the group's perspective, the next step in binding the new member to the group is either to recruit family and friends or to use their negative reactions to distance them. Sometimes the announcement actually comes in the form of total rift—a letter or phone call from an unknown place, informing the family that the member is gone.

During the honeymoon stage, focus on avoiding a complete breach. Almost all families have an initial, negative reaction to the member's announcement that she is leaving school, traveling to some faraway place, changing her name, or other radical decision. Some families and individuals respond calmly in time of crisis and can readily maintain their equilibrium. Others openly and immediately express shock and skepticism.

Whatever your temperament, try to recover from any early expressions of anger and dismay and avoid condemnation. Show interest in learning more about the group. Do NOT explain that you think this may be a cult. Do NOT ask your loved one if the group is a cult. Remember, your loved one is *in*, initiated, converted, and committed. He is extolling the advantages of his new life precisely because he is now securely within the group fold.

There is no good measure of how long the honeymoon lasts and the new cult member will not tell you, either. While she is committed to the group, she will support the group's position. One woman told her family after a successful exit counseling that she had almost immediately hated life in the group and longed to leave—yet she had consistently refused to visit or even talk to her family at that time.

The Veteran

After the honeymoon comes reality. The veteran has been a full member for some time—months at least, usually a year or more—and is expected to work hard for the group, raising money or turning over her income, recruiting new members, and laboring at various tasks.

The group's love is now conditional on the veteran's performance, and her compliance, or on the leader's pleasure. She has been punished and has seen others punished for failing to measure up. She has lied, cheated, or otherwise violated her integrity for the sake of the group.

She is keenly aware that things are not working out as promised, but still believes that the group is special and different. She thinks that the gap between her expectations and the flawed reality are her fault, the result of her personal shortcomings. She sees doubt or unhappiness as evidence of her own inadequacy and looks forward still to the day when her expectations of perfection will be fulfilled.

Appropriate, well-timed kindness and love will have an impact on someone at this stage, although it may not be immediately evident. A birthday card or flowers—if they reach her—will carry the message that there are people who remember and love her and don't think of her as someone who's not measuring up to expectations.

You may be able to arrange a visit or, if you have been visiting, a longer or better visit. You may hear words of doubt or hesitation. Don't pounce. Keep trying to make her more comfortable with you, so that she begins to think it might be safe to be with you and that you will not blame her for her uncertainties. A good guideline for visits is the Helen Hayes guideline. This great actress once described her goal for her audience as, "Always leave them wanting more." Try to make the family encounter so good that the cult member will regret when it's over.

The Habituated Member

The habituated member has been in the group for years and appears to be pretty thoroughly settled there. He knows what's going on, but rationalizes by telling himself that everyone is like that (constantly out to con and cheat). There may now be powerful incentives to keep him in the group. He may have advanced to a leadership level and may receive substantial pay-offs in power or money. He may have committed crimes, leaving himself subject to blackmail if he defects. He may be miserable in the group but so acculturated that it's very difficult to conceive of life outside the group. And, of course, a parent with children born of a cult marriage may have to face leaving children in the group with a cult-involved spouse.

Depending on how miserable he truly is, the habituated cult member may be more approachable than you know, for he is likely to conceal assiduously all signs of disaffection. This person may be considered more secure by the group than he really is, and may be allowed liberties, such as unchaperoned visits with the family, that for a less habituated member would be forbidden.

The key distinction between the veteran and the habituated stage is the disillusionment of the habituated cult member. While the veteran member has a vague notion that all is not well, she retains her faith in the revelation and the leader and tends to blame herself as the source of the problems.

The habituated member no longer expects great things of anyone. Fear of the leader and magical ideas about the dire consequences of leaving are important factors that keep him in the group, as is sheer habit, the human tendency to keep on doing what one is used to doing and knows how to do. The forces keeping the habituated member in the group are usually also practical and situational: If he leaves, where is he to go? What is he to do? His friends, and possibly other family members, his job and his housing may all be entangled with the group. He has little or no money and a distorted view of the outside world. In *Seductive Poison*, former People's Temple member Deborah Layton recounts the difficulties she faced in leaving Jonestown. They ranged from the wrenching decision that she could not take her ill mother with her, nor even tell her goodbye, to the practical difficulty of how to get to the airport.

A successful approach to the habituated member must address these concerns. It's probably no news to him that he is engaged in a destructive enterprise, though he may not comprehend the magnitude of the lies he's been told, nor will a clear demonstration of this necessarily move him to action. Rather, persuading him that he can surmount the obstacles, both psychological and material, that bar him from the outside world and, contrary to the group's dire predictions, live a better life, is the challenge.

Castaways

People not only leave cults, they get thrown out. These former members have come to be called "castaways." This can happen for various reasons: Sometimes the member's family has caused so much trouble for the group that the member is no longer worth the trouble of keeping him. (The castaway is usually told that his family has made it impossible for him to achieve salvation, or whatever). Sometimes the member is no longer useful due to illness or mental breakdown. Sometimes the member has violated important rules, exposed the group or the leader in some way, or is made the scapegoat for a disaster.

Whatever the reason for expulsion, it is not the member's choice and often seems to him a personal failure of overwhelming magnitude. People expelled from their groups usually do not understand that they have had a cult experience. They are highly susceptible to recruitment by another group and tend to be far more depressed than ex-members who leave of their own accord.

If you happen to know that your family member has been expelled from the group, and if you know how to reach her, this can be a golden opportunity—unless she was kicked out at your instigation, in which case she may never forgive you. You may not care about forgiveness, but be mindful that unless exit counseled, she may be ripe for recruitment by another group, and also that a severe depression is a possibility. When approaching someone who was expelled, use your best information about her stage of involvement at the time of the expulsion. It will improve your planning.

Awareness of the cult member's stage of involvement can be helpful, but there are no hard-and-fast rules about what to do when. Within every stage, there will be times of greater or lesser commitment. Sometimes the influence of the group will be shaky and the member's participation less than whole-hearted. There will be recollections of former goals and pleasures now forbidden. There will be punishments, trials, and abuse within the group. There may be awareness of corrupt or illegal activity. Long before he is ready to admit openly that joining the group was a mistake and that he wants out, the cult member may be secretly regretting his involvement and re-thinking his commitment.

In addition to assessing extrinsic factors, it is important to assess intrinsic factors—things unrelated to cult pressures and deceptions—that make membership appealing or unappealing to the member. These factors may relate either to the member's personality or to the member's situation at the time of recruitment. A person who has always enjoyed being different and startling people might find it very attractive to don a bizarre outfit or shave her head, for example. Or a person who is shy and self-conscious about dating might find comfort in a group where dating is forbidden.

These factors cut both ways. There will be things about the group that are intrinsically distasteful from day one. They may, over time, become increasingly important to the cult member—lack of privacy, boring and repetitive hard labor, or a punitive atmosphere—so that the positive factors weigh less. Changes outside the group may have an effect as well: A family that stops pressuring the former student to return to school, an unprecedented career opportunity, and so forth.

Use the MEMBER'S PRESENT SITUATION form to help sort out these important factors. As you work through the form, remember that what matters is how the *cult member* feels, not how *you* feel or what *you* like.

The categories suggested on the form are necessarily very general. Use your knowledge of the member to identify "Other" attractions and repulsions or to revise the categories so they fit better. For instance, "new friends" is listed as an attraction to the group. But if the member has been in the cult for years, an attraction to the group might be "old friends," rather than "new friends." Some of the attractions of the group might reflect unflatteringly on the member. For example, he may be snobbish and enjoy the sense of elitism he draws from the group.

As with all the other forms, make extra copies of the MEMBER'S PRESENT SITUATION before you fill it out. Re-work the form from time to time if circumstances change or you acquire additional information. When you have filled it out as best you can, you will have a focus that may suggest some avenues of approach.

This particular exercise may have a depressing effect if you find there are many attractions to the cult and few to the outside world, but this is not a balance sheet. A single factor on one side may outweigh all the factors on the other side.

Cults do not like illness, for example. It is inconvenient, depriving them of the services the member should be providing. It is often ideologically inappropriate, since members of the elite are not supposed to get sick. The need for medical care is a financial drain if the cult member is uninsured. If the illness was brought on or exacerbated by the lifestyle and practices of the group, the situation may result in unpleasant publicity or even criminal charges. If the member is hospitalized or unable to work for any length of time, the rest and proper food may give her the time and opportunity to think—and she may start thinking.

Illness may actually cause the group to send the member home, sometimes in shocking condition. Steven Hassan writes about how he was sent home by the Unification Church after being hospitalized following an accident. In another case, a young man with a serious chronic illness stopped taking his medication after joining the group. His father threatened the group with a lawsuit should any ill befall his son as a consequence, and the group sent him home.

This is tantamount to exile for the cult member, however, not exit. After you have attended to the medical aspects of the case, you will need to help the cult member deal with severe emotional confusion, probably beginning with exit counseling.

This chapter and those preceding it have dealt with specific, objective information—history, behavior, and knowledge about the cult member. Having learned as much as you could about WHAT happened, it is time to focus on HOW it happened.

Date: _____

MEMBER'S PRESENT SITUATION

Check each item below that applies to the person you want to help. Then review the items you have checked and highlight those where family and/or friends might do something to influence change. Number the highlighted items in order of their importance to the member.

ATTRACTIONS TO GROUP

_____ new friends

_____ new skills

_____ economic security

_____ unconventional life

_____ idealistic goals

_____ spiritual activities

_____ sense of belonging

_____ sense of elitism

_____ dependency on leader

Other: _____

_____

_____

ATTRACTIONS TO OUTSIDE WORLD

_____ old friends

_____ long-held interests and hobbies

_____ family

_____ traditional customs and values

_____ career development

_____ free time

_____ financial independence

_____ privacy

_____ material goods and pleasures

Other: _____

_____

_____

REPULSIONS FROM OUTSIDE WORLD

_____ family conflicts

_____ dislike of materialistic society

_____ doubts and anxieties about career choices

_____ doubts and anxieties about dating/ sexuality

_____ pressure to compete

_____ recent loss, rejection, or failure

_____ loneliness, difficulty making friends

Other: _____

_____

REPULSIONS FROM GROUP

_____ interpersonal conflicts with other members

_____ conflicts with leaders

_____ demands of group to conform

_____ doubts about doctrines or practices

_____ abuse

_____ discovery of cheating or deception

_____ illness

Other: _____

_____

Chapter Six
Understanding Cult Involvement

Think of a favorite movie. Think of the first time you saw that movie, how you bought your ticket and settled into your seat, how the lights dimmed, and how, when the feature came on, you became more and more absorbed in the story. The actions and pictures on the screen overwhelmed your senses until—although, abstractly, you knew you were sitting in a dark room with dozens of people around you—you were far more aware of the illusion on the screen than the reality of the theater.

That is an experience of an altered state of consciousness, one that most of us have had. Remember how you felt when the movie ended, the lights went up and with a jolt, you were back in a theatre crowded with people? That was your return to reality.

Have you ever bought something you had no intention of buying? Or have you bought something that you indeed wanted and needed, but paid far more than you had intended to spend? Have you ever gone along with a group somewhere you really didn't want to go (maybe because you didn't want to anger someone you cared about or didn't want to be a "party-pooper")? Some people are more susceptible to pressures like these, some less so. But it is a rare human being, indeed, who has *never* succumbed to subtle persuasion or group pressure.

Many aspects of cult involvement relate to ordinary human experiences that all of us have, experiences that in appropriate measure and settings are not harmful and may even be helpful. De-mystifying these experiences will help you understand what has happened to your loved one and re-establish strained or broken connections. This chapter focuses on a practical understanding of the phenomenon called "thought reform," "mind control," or, my preferred term, "mind-bending."

Let's start with two major points:

1.   What has trapped your loved one is an amalgam of influence techniques, long known and used by con men and others all over the world to make people do things they wouldn't otherwise do. Most of these techniques are intensified versions of sales and persuasion techniques we see daily and might even use ourselves. Some may induce altered states of consciousness.

BUT cult members don't see it that way.

2.   Your loved one has had a deeply moving, personal, emotional experience that convinces him or her that the leader's revelation is genuine. The cult member is—metaphorically speaking— caught up in the thrilling drama. The group and the member will do everything they can to prevent the "show" from ending and the lights from going up.

Stir it all together: the focus and thrill of the movie, the urgency, glibness and persuasiveness of the high-pressure salesman, and the group pressures of your companions of the moment. Subtract the reality checks. The lights won't go up, the music won't resolve in a finale and the credits won't roll. Instead of ending after a couple of hours, this show's duration is unlimited. Finally, suppose that what you are being sold is a compelling idea that appeals to your idealism, your quest for spiritual fulfillment, or simply your desire to be a more successful person. This will approximate the atmosphere of a cult conversion.

Much of the stigma attached to cult involvement stems from the notion that there is something wrong with the person recruited.

        "Sam's too smart to get fooled by this stuff!"

Or,

        "Brenda comes from a solid, middle-class background. Nobody in our family is crazy,"

are the kinds of responses family members often make.

Actually, intelligence—good powers of concentration, a good memory, and a good imagination— may make people more susceptible to this kind of manipulation and trickery. Nor is mental illness a pre-requisite. Although some cult members do have a history of mental problems, the number is probably no greater than those in the general population who have mental problems.

The research on cult involvement suggests that people get inducted into destructive cults because they are vulnerable and in a situation that leaves them open to the recruitment process. They may be strangers in town, lacking friends and social activities. They may be searchers, looking for a richer spiritual or material life. They may have recently suffered a major loss, such as job or spouse. Or a boss or a friend may pressure them, seeming to place a job or friendship at risk if they don't attend meetings of the group. There have been cases, for instance, when a residential advisor in a college dormitory pressured a freshman to attend a "Bible study" group.

"Mind bending," as it is more accurately called in Canada, is a truer description of this condition than "mind control," because the cult convert's mind is never one hundred percent "controlled." Outside of the areas where thinking and beliefs are distorted by demands of the group, cult converts do not lose their professional skills or their language abilities or even their rational thinking capacity.

It is not necessary to discuss mind-bending techniques specifically and at length (and if you are interested, you can easily find information from some of the resources listed at the end of this book), but do keep these points in mind:

- These techniques are in constant use because they work well on all human beings. Your son, daughter, spouse, relative or friend was not stupid, heedless, or demented because he fell for them. He fell for them because he was human and either had the ill luck to encounter them when he was unusually open to influence or because they were specifically tailored to appear to sell what he was looking for (or both).

- Mind-bending techniques as practiced by destructive cults often involve manipulation and deception, as well as intense persuasion.

- "Unbending" a mind that's been "bent," is a complicated process that is not likely to happen overnight and is not likely to happen spontaneously. Even though most cult members who leave do so on their own, most are bewildered about what happened and will often suffer personal difficulties until they get help.

- It's tough to convince any human being to change. The bigger the change, the tougher it is. Although the change may have been fraudulently induced, it is real change. Persuading someone to disengage from a cult means getting him to abandon a major commitment to which he has dedicated his life.

Depending on their level of involvement, cult members may or may not know they've been manipulated. Long-time members may be in on the scam, excusing it on the grounds that they are doing it for a higher purpose. Or disillusioned cult members may justify their behavior on the grounds that "everybody does it," and this is the way the world works.

Yet, at the time of joining, most cult members have had a transforming inner experience, a revelation that they interpret as validation of the leader's claims. With this acceptance, they joined the world of magic:

- A member of a New Age meditation group saw the leader surrounded by a golden cloud.

- A member of a psychotherapy cult saw her leader walk through walls.

- A former member of a Bible group described what he calls "the buzz," a continuous high that sustained his conviction of the rightness of the leader's teaching.

The experience crosses all ideologies and all types of cults.

What has happened? The experience itself is genuine. But all too often it was not, as the recruit believes, spontaneous or self-generated. It was in many cases deliberately induced from without, usually with the help of fraud, trickery, and deception. Most people have no idea how suggestible we are and how easily our senses can be tricked. A moderately skilled hypnotist can make a whole roomful of people see things that aren't there. Sleep deprivation alone will eventually cause hallucinations and delusions.

So universal is our suggestibility that medical researchers routinely measure the "placebo effect" when testing new treatments. One group of the people in the test believes they are getting the new treatment, although they actually are not. Inevitably, many in this group improve. To demonstrate the effectiveness of the treatment, researchers must show that significantly more of the people improve who actually got the treatment than those who got the placebo.

Cults generally use a variety of manipulative techniques. The recruit may be short on sleep, short on protein, bombarded by believers, and victimized by tricks ranging from misuse of hypnosis to "telepathy." Confused and bemused, the recruit is kept busy, tired, and surrounded by other members. There is very little opportunity for reflecting on the cult's ideas and activities.

One reason destructive groups often demand secrecy about the recruit's involvement is to prevent friends and relatives from raising questions while the prospect's mind is still relatively clear. Uplifted by an overwhelming sensory experience, cult recruits are kept off balance, and prevented, in effect, from going home or to any other place where reason might set in.

The transforming experience may come earlier or later in the recruitment process and may be more critical and dramatic in some groups than in others. In some cases, where a person's involvement is marginal, or the group is heavily focused on commercial activity, the transformation may not happen. Or it may happen in a modified form in which the members feel caught up in an innovative, exciting, creative way of doing things. By and large, it does happen and not only to one person. All the members of the group have comparable experiences.

Once the recruit accepts this personal experience as confirmation of the leader's authenticity, his acceptance of the leader's authority increases significantly and, in some cases, may be absolutely unquestioning.

For instance, the leader of a large meditation group tells members that they can fly. Although members practice long and hard, the most anyone has ever actually achieved is a series of hops across a room. But this does not discourage them. Members see the hops as "short flights." One former member of this group relates that during this experience, he felt himself take off and then "land" on the opposite side of the room and had no awareness of the intermediate "hops" he took. One day, these devotees believe, they will fly longer and longer distances. Their compelling meditative experiences have convinced them of the leader's authority. When they fail at "flying," they will tend, with help from the group's leadership of course, to blame themselves, rather than question the leader. They may say, for example, that they are not yet spiritually advanced enough to "fly."

A person who has given up thinking can easily accept that a loud boom is the voice of God talking to the leader, even though it's coming from a kettle drum; or that "mind over matter" applies even to such situations as brain tumors; or that by eating discarded food from trash bins, she is saving the environment.

You can tell such a person anything. You can tell him that if it feels good, it must be *right*, whether "it" is drug-induced hallucinations, having a sexual encounter with the leader, or hypnotic emptiness. Or you can tell him that if it feels good, like eating your favorite food, it must be *wrong*, because our feelings are temptations of Satan.

The perception of the leader's magic power also reinforces the dread of terrible consequences for those who leave. If, after this clear demonstration of the truth, you turn your back on it, there is no saving you. If it is a Bible group you renounce, you're clearly going to burn in Hell. If it is a group whose collective powers of meditation are saving the world, your defection harms the whole world. If it is a militia or survival group, you are heading out to a world ruled by enemies who are waiting to arrest, torture, or otherwise overwhelm you.

Unless and until the cult member is ready to listen to information that explains and reinterprets this compelling experience, it is futile and counterproductive to try to explain it away or to question the beliefs that grow from this delusion. By definition, a belief is something that can neither be proved nor disproved. Core beliefs tend not to be subject to reason, and your attack on the member's beliefs will be met by a withering counter attack on your beliefs. An all-powerful God created the universe? Prove it. There is no God and everything that happens is by chance? Prove it.

You will be told that great spiritual leaders (or innovators) inevitably face the scorn and antagonism of the establishment, that you are closed-minded and unwilling to entertain new possibilities and that your skepticism simply demonstrates the distance between you and the cult member. This is a no-win discussion. In fact, you are probably reinforcing the cult member's affiliation by showing him how effective are the responses he has been taught.

Because beliefs are a highly emotional topic, you also risk saying something you will later regret and you risk providing the cult member with a reason to cut you off. The chapter on *Communicating with Cults Members* has more on how to handle ideological discussions.

In addition to the high-pressure influence techniques and the transformative, internal experience, powerful forces of group dynamics are operating on the cult member.

We are all members of numerous groups, and our participation in these groups is an important part of our identity: "I'm a Jones," we may say, or "I'm a Methodist," "I'm a teenager," and so forth, meaning, I am one of a group of people named Jones, I am one of a group that subscribes to the Methodist faith, I am one of the group aged 13-19.

Much of our identity with particular groups is not within our control, but simply relates to the circumstances of our life: our age, gender, place and time of birth, for example. Especially in the United States, other important group affiliations are more likely to result from our own personal choice: occupation and employment, hobbies, and religious affiliations are examples of these.

Groups behave differently from individuals. People in groups do things they would not do on their own:

- Groups loosen our inhibitions. An angry individual student is not likely to camp in the Dean's office shaking his fist and demanding a meeting. An angry group of students is more likely to do this.

- Groups intensify our emotions. Have you ever found yourself cheering madly for a team that you don't care much about because everyone around you is cheering madly?

- Groups affect our judgment. If all your friends are proclaiming what a great movie you just saw, while you thought it boring, you are likely to soften your criticism (unless you are one of those folks who enjoys opposing, in which case you're likely to be even more critical).

- Groups acting together can achieve more than individuals. A group that organizes around a specific project, whether it's fund-raising, revolution, or painting a house, gets more done and has more fun than the same number of individuals acting on their own.

Companionship is a basic human need. (That is why solitary confinement is such a terrible punishment.) People need group involvement, with family and community, to function well. From church groups to music and sports groups, to political groups, to co-workers' groups, people who come together for a common purpose have a solid ground for liking each other and derive satisfaction that is not attainable on their own. If you have ever worked hard to elect a school board member and won, if you have ever been part of a trophy-winning team, or of a choir that turned in a stellar performance, you will know the rich satisfaction that rewarded the group's effort.

The other side of this coin is how distressing it is to be rejected by a group you'd like to join—to be told your singing isn't good enough or that you are too old, or too young, or any other reason. It is worse to be thrown out of a group—to be put off the team because your performance was disappointing or because you have violated some major rule, for instance. This is one reason why it is so devastating to be fired from a job.

In a cult, these manifestations of group dynamics are effective both in recruitment and retention. Because the group consists of the chosen few who know the "secret," membership is more important and more meaningful than in other groups. Because the group loosens inhibitions, members are more likely to do things that in other settings their consciences would forbid. Because group endorsement blurs judgment, members are more likely to continue to accept the group's interpretations. Because the group enhances feelings, members are less likely to reflect.

Finally, as cult involvement cuts the member off from the world, the group replaces all his other connections—friends, family, and colleagues—and becomes his only source of companionship. To lose the group, then, is to lose a world: beliefs, friends, family, occupation, housing, and even employment may all be lost, depending upon the nature of the group involvement.

Now, add human inertia to all this. All of us put up with a lot, every day, because somehow, it's easier to bear with it than to change. We put up with things: the warped hinge that makes it hard to open the gate; the lazy co-worker whom we cover up for; the spouse whose heavy drinking is getting more and more worrisome. Sometimes we tell ourselves we can't do anything about it. (This is true often enough to be a terrific excuse.). Sometimes the risk of failure is more than we want to chance. Sometimes we grow accustomed to a situation and don't notice how bad things are as it gradually grows worse. Sometimes we pretend the problem will just go away by itself, and that it won't happen again.

To sum up, the following factors bring people into cults and keep them there:

- Age-old, highly effective persuasion techniques have brought them in.
- The group appeals to some of their deepest desires and dreams.
- Each member has probably had a transforming emotional experience.
- The group meets basic needs for companionship and involvement.
- It is hard to change, even when we're in a bad situation.

Yet people do leave, often without any outside assistance, because the dream wears off, the situation becomes unbearably painful, or something startles them into seeing the deception. The following chapters will help you think about what you can do to encourage change.

Chapter Seven
Communicating with Cult Members

Communicating with a cult-involved family member can be a nerve-wracking exercise in frustration and anguish. Even a simple, "Hi, honey, how are you?" can provoke a tirade about how nosy and "controlling" you are—if you're skillful and lucky enough to get your loved one on the phone to begin with. Because it breaks the member's isolation and opens a door to the world outside, communication is precisely what the cult seeks to discourage.

The importance that abusive groups place on communication is obvious from the measures they take to obstruct it. The cult may limit members' access to telephones, monitor conversations, or demonize families as dangers to the salvation or physical well being of the cult member. Some groups hide their members. Others straightforwardly order members not to communicate. Cult members usually have little or no opportunity to talk privately with family or old friends. They are almost always with other cult members, even on visits home.

When you talk on the phone, cult-appointed monitors may be listening on the line. You may note frequent interruptions, with your family member saying, "Just a minute," while whispering to someone in the background. You may hear someone yelling cues—"You're over 21! Why are you letting her boss you around?" Many families suspect or know that mail is not delivered, or is censored before delivery.

Despite all this, opportunities occur—censored, chaperoned, or sporadic though they may be. Enhanced communications skills—even if, for the present, communication is a distant dream—will help you prepare for the hoped-for day when your loved one is ready to talk.

Remember these important points when you communicate with a cult member:

• The cultist doesn't see himself or herself as a victim, but as a winner, initiate into a powerful, select group and a disciple of spiritual giants. Of course, he's going to devote himself heart and soul to the Cause.

• Because he *knows* the Truth, anyone who disagrees with the cultist is either a mindless idiot or an agent of the Dark Side.

- Because he's now in Magic Land, association with anyone who disagrees might dim or pollute the purity of his faith. The cult member is encouraged to disentangle him- or herself from worldly drags on progress.

- Things that seem important to those on the outside—going back to school or work, showing up for Thanksgiving or sister's wedding or Grandpa's funeral—simply pale to insignificance against the vibrant excitement of the group's activities.

The cult member is primed to recruit people to the group and to ward off other information. She will have plenty to say to you. It is important that you *receive* her communications in a way that keeps the door open for continuing communication. It is hard—extremely hard and sometimes impossibly hard—to *listen*, to receive and process information when your dearly loved child, spouse, or friend is talking hurtful nonsense. Nevertheless, try to focus on listening to the person, not the nonsense.

Listening pays off in many ways:

- It shows you respect the speaker.
- You can get useful information about your family member and the group.
- It contradicts group propaganda about your closed mind and angry or controlling behavior.
- It keeps you connected.

If you can listen, it is more likely that you, in turn, will eventually be listened to. Your goal is both to convey messages and to hear messages.

It may help to remember that *listening* is not the same as agreeing.

> "Reverend Q is a flawless human being," one young woman (call her Elaine) told her mother.

The obvious answer is that no one is a flawless human being. But Elaine already knows that's what her mother thinks. "No-one's perfect" has been a household staple all of Elaine's life. She's persuaded—and is asserting—that Reverend Q is an exception to the rule. She is sharing something very important—something miraculous—with her mother. To answer, "Come now, dear, nobody's perfect," may be solid common sense, but it also demonstrates that her mother did not "get it," namely, the message about Reverend Q's miraculous nature.

Elaine's mother now has a chance to communicate, to convey the message that she "got it." One response that shows she is listening is simply to ask for more information. Something like,

"That's incredible! Tell me more about Reverend Q,"

will acknowledge the amazing nature of the information. Of course, she must be careful not to speak sarcastically or condescendingly. And, in the face of such a remarkable assertion, Elaine's mother should not go right on washing dishes or sipping her coffee as if her daughter had made some observation about the weather.

Alternatively, simply reflecting back the statement:

"Reverend Q must really be different,"

also signifies that one is listening.

Or one can reflect the emotional content of the message:

"You must feel uplifted to be with someone like Reverend Q."

These answers meet two important requirements:

1.   They acknowledge the importance of the assertion about Reverend Q.
2.   They accept the offer of a topic and the possibility of exploring it.

A good listener may also ask questions, so long as they're not designed to support a personal agenda that conflicts with the speaker's agenda:

"How often does Reverend Q preach?" is OK.

"What does Reverend Q preach about?" may produce significant information.

Avoid challenges.

"How do you know Reverend Q is a flawless human being?"

sounds like an attack, although a respectful,

> "Tell me how you came to realize that,"

could open a gold mine of information.

Sometimes, questions will indicate your desire to be a good listener, even if you didn't grasp the right intention:

> Are you telling me that there's something really different about Reverend Q?"

might sound a little skeptical, but at least you're checking.

Try to maintain the "good listener" stance even in the face of provocative messages such as,

> "Don't you know you're damned? You'll burn in Hell!"

These messages of rejection are called "thought-stoppers," because they disrupt communication that might lead the cult member to re-think her involvement. They are also intended to shock and alienate you and to distract everyone (not least, the cult member) from whatever subject triggered the thought-stopper.

Each group has its own "thought-stoppers." Learn to recognize those used by your group and develop a variety of constructive responses. You might simply refuse to take the bait, answering something like:

> "That's interesting, tell me why you think that."

Or you might turn the message around:

> "Well, if you're worrying about that, you must still love me and I'm glad of that."

Prepare yourself ahead of time and try to curb yourself when you feel the adrenalin rising. Calm, reflective thinking is your ally and the cult's enemy. Don't ignore your emotions, but remember how easy it is for others—particularly those who know you well—to manipulate your emotions. And remember how much it is in your interest to stay in control, especially when someone else is trying to upset you.

While you cannot control what someone else says or does to you, you can control your response. One good way to put a guard on your words is to frame your responses as "I" messages. An "I" message focuses on how you feel or what you think about something, rather than stating your opinion of the thing or person.

Use "I" messages to express your own thoughts and feelings about the cult member's words and deeds:

> " I felt very hurt when you didn't come to Grandpa's funeral."

or

> "It bothers me a lot that I can't see you alone."

Use them to respond to threats and pressure to join, contribute, or otherwise support the group:

> "I understand that this is very important to you, but I'm not ready to do this yet."

An "I" message may be a good response to a thought-stopper.

> "You're not my mother!"

naturally evokes an emotional reaction:

> "How can you say that!" or

> "That is a terrible, hurtful thing to say!"

If you respond by saying calmly:

> "When you say that, I feel very hurt because I gave birth to you and took care of you all these years and I love you very much,"

you are raising topics of great import without attacking the speaker.

Reject the temptation to respond emotionally—either with sorrow or with anger—to shrill or angry demands. Don't hesitate, if you are getting overwrought, to take a time-out:

"I'm getting very upset with this conversation. I need some time to think about this before we go on. I'll call you back later."

Use "I" messages to try to move from ultimatum to negotiation:

"I respect your right to your own beliefs and your own way of life, and I'm asking you to respect my right to the same."

Use "I" messages to accede to a demand:

"I'm sorry that my letter upset you. I love you and I want to be in touch and I won't criticize the group again,"

or to refuse:

"I love you very much, but I don't endorse the group's goals, so I won't support it financially."

If the member threatens that he will cut off contact unless you send money, join the group, or stop some activity he disapproves of, use an "I" message:

"I love you very much and no matter how much we disagree, I will never cut off contact with you. Any time you get in touch, I will be happy to hear from you."

If the member indeed cuts off contact, he will have your affirmation ringing in his ears. Continue to write letters and place phone calls, even though they may be rejected, so he can see that you meant it.

Plan your communications ahead of time. Know what you want to communicate. Be aware of what you are communicating and how you are communicating it. Think long and hard about what messages are most important. Keep in mind all the information you have gathered about the cult member, the cult, and yourselves. Remember that your goal is to encourage the cult member back to the outside world. Use your assessment of the MEMBER'S PRESENT SITUATION. What will attract him? What will scare or repel him?

The best communications are clear and brief. Clear and brief communications are not necessarily easy to prepare, especially in complex situations. Jean Monnet, founder of the economic coalition that led to the European Union, often worked through nineteen or more drafts as he distilled complex concepts into clear, understandable language. He demanded clarity, accuracy, and simplicity to assure that all parties understood his proposals.

You, similarly, want to convey messages that cannot be misunderstood, messages you must send through a fog of cult-induced confusion. You need clarity, accuracy, and simplicity so that your loved one will hear you say, "I love you," or "You are safe with me."

Once you have decided on your basic messages, plan different ways of communicating them, both in words and non-verbally. You can say, "I love you," by a hug or a look if you are with a person, by letter or card, by telephone if you are not. You can say it long distance without words by sending a favorite treat on a birthday (if the group's dietary rules allow), sending flowers, photos, newspaper clippings, by traveling a long way for a short visit, or by other gestures that show your care and concern. The worksheet, SENDING IMPORTANT MESSAGES, suggests some important messages and provides an opportunity to plan how you will convey them.

Think about the situation and the cult member's perspective. Your approach will be quite different if you are attempting to re-open communications after a breach of several years than if you are dealing with someone who still lives at home but is spending all her income and some of yours on weekend and evening courses and is pressuring you to do the same.

Be patient. Perhaps the first thing you need to do is reassure the cult member that she can safely communicate without being attacked or harangued about her cult affiliation. Establishing a relationship through small talk or brief notes about family or local events may be the most that you can realistically expect at this point. Sometimes people who are unwilling to write or call their families will speak with or write to trusted family friends. Eventually, this channel of communication may lead to direct communication.

Communication may be for sale. You may find that the cult member will call or write in return for a stipend. There is no simple answer to this. You don't want to subsidize your loved one's involvement with the group. But you do want to hear his voice regularly, to know that he is still alive and within reach of a telephone and able to have the opportunity to share family news. How much money does he want? How readily can you spare this amount? Have you any assurance how the money will be used? Will this become a kind of blackmail, with the price rising at regular intervals?

Ask yourselves all the questions you can think of when you are struggling with a choice like this. Make sure your negotiations spell out clearly what your limits are and that you set limits you can enforce. What will happen if the cult member misses a call? If he does not call at the agreed time and so "misses" you? How long or short a conversation is acceptable? Avoid stipulations you cannot enforce, such as requesting that the conversations be private.

Of all possible approaches, opposing the cult member's beliefs, affiliations and activities is the least likely to work. Beliefs are deeply felt. Remember the overwhelming inner experience the member has probably had. Telling people they are wrong or crazy or stupid or misled or have gotten caught up in a cult is a good way to keep them tightly wrapped in their convictions. The cult member has been primed to deal with these arguments and has some powerful responses on his side. It is unlikely that you can change anyone's beliefs by attacking them, although you can certainly irritate and alienate the believer. In fact, you may actually reinforce the group's beliefs by causing the member to restate them over and over.

In the United States, where freedom of speech and freedom of religion are so highly prized, the law protects freedom of belief. A person may believe that in a previous life she was Queen Cleopatra. Atheists may believe that everything came into existence by accident and happenstance. Voodoo adherents may believe that their priests can command the spirits of evil. By attacking the cult member's beliefs, you merely open the way for him to point out how vulnerable your own beliefs are, and how closed-minded and "controlling" (by trying to talk him out of his beliefs) you are.

Since the group's practices stem from its beliefs, you are equally unlikely to succeed in arguments about what is wrong with these practices. If a person believes that by wearing green he can fend off evil, he will wear green. If he believes that the world will end next week, he won't be working on college applications, home improvements, or other projects directed toward the future. Once the recruit has accepted that Reverend Moon is the Messiah or that Minister Z has the only correct interpretation of the Bible or that The Teacher is in touch with beings from outer space, the rest follows with inescapable logic.

When you talk with a cult member, the conversation will probably turn to beliefs because the cult member has typically been trained to assert his beliefs aggressively. You might want to take the opportunity to learn more about them, provided you can confine your reaction to careful listening and exploratory questions.

If pressed to comment, you might respond that, although you disagree, you will not attack his beliefs, as he doubtless has his reasons for adopting them and you respect his right to have them. You might talk about how people whose ideas were initially scorned, like Copernicus when he asserted that the earth goes around the sun, were later proven correct. Rather than talking about your own beliefs, talk about the importance of respecting other people's beliefs and, when discussing beliefs, to be tolerant of differences. Your ability to listen will help the cult member feel respected.

If pushed to express an opinion, stay with "I" messages:

> "I'm not convinced," or
> "I'm still comfortable with my old beliefs,"

does not attack the speaker or the speaker's assertion. It simply states your position. The cult member really can't quarrel with this because it is your own report of your personal position.

This is much less threatening than, "I still say it's garbage," which attacks the cult member's beliefs, or "You're crazy!" which attacks the person herself.

This temperate approach will also pay off when you are fending off recruitment attempts. It's rational to say,

> "If respect for your beliefs is open-minded on my part, don't you need also to respect my beliefs?"

You may also be able to point out the double standard he sets when he demands that you respect or support his belief while he may freely heap scorn on yours.

Communications may be both verbal (in words) and non-verbal. Even when we express ourselves through words, our tone of voice, attitude, and body language are part of the communication. People are often unaware of their non-verbal communications, and may convey contradictory messages. For example:

"How interesting," you say, without looking up from the TV.

"I don't care what you do!" as tears are rolling down your face.

"You are the most important person in the world to me," glancing at your watch to make sure you won't be late to your next appointment.

These messages are confusing. They may be honest, in that you are confused or conflicted, but they confuse the recipient and give him or her the option of noting only the negative and ignoring the positive element.

Sometimes people are deliberately insincere in the hope of avoiding unpleasant consequences. But "I'm not angry," pronounced in a cold voice with a tight face and hard exhalation of breath, is not convincing and opens you to the charge of "lying." If you are a professional actor (or are dealing with someone who doesn't know you well), you may be able not to look angry when in fact you are angry.

It's usually best to come up with an honest, though non-inflammatory answer,

"Yes, when you say I'm going to Hell, I do feel angry, and hurt, too."

All high-pressure salespeople, from the telemarketer to the mind bender, want you to buy NOW, before you have time to think—and with good reason. Your loved one's judgment and powers of reasoning have been largely replaced by simple slogans and black-and-white responses. Shape your communications to promote thoughtful reflection, that response of the brain that says, "Wait a minute, I'm not sure what this is all about."

For example, cults often portray our society as one that over-values thinking and reasoning and de-values our emotions. If you are accused of this, tactfully point out the over-simplification. Parents (and other loved ones) do pressure family members to do things they think are "sensible," despite the person's own preference. A young woman may, under family pressure, enroll in engineering school, even though she really wants to be a singer. And she may be very unhappy about it. But her decision was driven by a strong emotional element—her ties to her family—not just a rational judgment about the risk inherent in attempting a career as a singer. We can acknowledge that this is a conflicted situation and we can also point out that the family is truly trying to act in their family member's best interests and is thinking ultimately of her happiness.

It is certainly unbalanced to disregard our feelings, but our feelings are often conflicted and sometimes they are misleading. It is also unbalanced to disregard our ability to think—to measure, reason, and judge. To function effectively, people need to use both feeling and thinking.

Note the difference between "responding" and "reacting." The saying, "Refrain until you can respond, rather than react," is credited to *samurai* training. This is a good guideline for communications with cult-involved family members. If a phone call or demand takes you by surprise, don't let yourself be pressured or rushed. If you need to think, say so.

Perhaps the most difficult time to remember this is when you're faced with a "thought-stopper." Thought-stoppers may be inflammatory words, as described above, or activities, such as chanting, speaking in tongues, screaming, or running out of the room. Cult members use these behaviors to avoid getting involved in conversations that might move them away from the group. Verbal thought-stoppers were discussed earlier in this chapter.

How best can you deal with non-verbal thought-stoppers like chanting? As always, this depends on the people involved and the situation.

You might simply wait until the chanting stops and then inquire,

> "I'm interested that you were inspired to chant just now—can you tell me more about that?"

Another way to deal with thought stopping is simply to ignore it and respond with your own message. A father once asked his cult-involved daughter a question that triggered a tirade about angry, cold, controlling, closed-minded, obsolete, and doomed people, ending with, "You're not my father!" When the recruit finally stopped for breath, the father looked wistfully at his daughter and said, "You know what? I love you."

Dealing with thought-stoppers is a good way to use your expertise about yourselves and the cult member. What triggered the thought-stopper? A topic? A time of day? A hint of opposition? Knowing the cult member as you do, what is the best way to avoid triggering thought-stoppers? Knowing yourself, what is the best way to keep them from throwing you off the track?

Another obstacle to communicating with cult members is the group's jargon, which often ascribes different meanings to what we think of as ordinary words. The chapter, "About the Group" discusses group jargon. It is helpful and appropriate to use the jargon. Using "groupspeak" implies that you accept the cult member's decision and shows that you are open to change. This may be very important down the line if you want the cult member to be open to change.

> If the member asks you to use his new name, use it.

> If a trip home is "travel to the outer world," ask when he will be able to travel to the outer world.

> If he characterizes selling flowers in airports as "fund-raising," ask him how the fund-raising is coming.

The worksheet, USING THE PRIVATE LANGUAGE, gives you some drill in using the group's jargon.

Watch out for terms that may sound to you like metaphors, but are literal truth to the cult member. A minister may urge his congregants to "come home" to the Lord, meaning that they can become more spiritually comfortable by adhering to a belief or course of action. But the cult member who urges his sister to "Come home," may mean a geographic place—"Come to headquarters"—because "home" is where the leader is.

When this kind of jargon gets into the conversation, be sure to make your answer clear:

> "To me, home is where I am now because I don't adhere to Guru's teachings. But I would love to visit you, if that's what you're suggesting."

What if the cult member (it can happen) expresses some hesitancy about his own convictions? Don't jump on it: "Thank God! You're waking up at last!" Help him explore his feelings:

"Can you tell me more about what's bothering you?" or

"I don't know. How would you check that out?"

It might be appropriate to help the member get other sources of information, such as assisting with a Web search or talking to someone who has information about the group. Encourage him, calmly and quietly, to question and think. If you are planning an exit counseling, this might be the signal that the member is ready.

Conversations with a cult-involved family member are sometimes disjointed or incoherent. Cult members may go off into long wandering digressions instead of responding to questions. They can be moody and inconsistent. One family found that their cult-involved daughter might call up and harangue them one week and the next week be perfectly calm and friendly.

Cult members have moments of both greater adherence to and greater disaffection from the group. You're not likely to know if your call or letter arrived at one of these moments, but the response might reflect it. That's why it's important to keep reaching out, no matter how disinterested or angry the cult member may seem. Consistency is one of the attractions you can offer.

To hone your communications skills, look at the exercise, LISTENING AND RESPONDING. This will help you learn how to interpret some typical cult-inspired remarks in the light of the group's beliefs and practices. You can then develop responses that will keep the communications coming.

You don't have to confine yourselves to working on the remarks in the form. If there are other remarks you want to deal with, use this formula to prepare them. Practice both the remarks and your responses out loud and take turns both as speaker and responder to see how the remarks and your answers affect you.

For some people, applying their already good communications skills to the cult situation will not be particularly difficult. Others may need considerable time to master and incorporate these skills into the emotionally charged encounters with the cult member. Do what you can when you can do it. Review your conversations with the cult member and try to distinguish what worked and what didn't so that each succeeding encounter will be more successful than the previous one. Apply these methods in interactions with other people so you will become more comfortable using them. Good communication may be the critical element in noting opportunities and in taking advantage of them.

SENDING IMPORTANT MESSAGES

Message to communicate	Strategies for communicating (both verbal and non-verbal)
a. I (we) love you and always will.	1. 2. 3.
b. We want to share family joys and sorrows with you.	1. 2. 3.
c. We have no intention of harming you, physically or psychologically.	1. 2. 3.
d. We respect your right to be different from us - even to reject beliefs and ideals we hold very dear.	1. 2. 3.
e. You will be safe with us.	1. 2. 3.
f. If you ever come to us in need, we will help you all we can.	1. 2. 3.

USING THE PRIVATE LANGUAGE

Translate the sentence into "groupspeak" and write it in the space provided. Practice saying it until you are fluent. Imagine some possible answers and your followup remarks.

English	*Groupspeak*
1. Tell me about the group's dietary rules.	
2. What is the group's goal?	
3. What is the reason for your (choose one): hairdo, clothing, avoidance of _____ ?	
4. What do you do for relaxation and amusement?	
5. I'd like to hear more about the group's ideas.	
6. It would mean a lot to us if you could come home for Christmas.	
7. I'm not likely ever to join the group, but I don't see why we can't be close in other respects.	
8. What do you like best about the group?	
9. Your brother's feelings are very hurt because you didn't come to his wedding.	
10. I don't understand how this fits in with your job (or school) commitments.	

LISTENING AND RESPONDING

The first column below lists some of the typical statements you are likely to hear from a cult-involved family member. Listen to the message, and write an interpretation of it in the second column. Then write a non-hostile response in the third column. The first is already done as an example.

Remark	Interpretation	Response
You're an evildoer!	If you're not on our side, you're on the enemy's side.	I'm sorry if I've offended you. Please tell me why you say that.
I'm sorry if you have cancer, but you brought it on yourself.		
That's an impure thought and you're trying to pollute me!		
If you really love me, you'd send money for the mission.		
You say you want me to come home to my family, but this is my home and family		
Guru knows the truth.		
I can't come for the wedding. I have important things to do here.		
If you say (or do) that, you'll never speak to me again!		

Chapter Eight
Finding a Missing Person

"You are an Obstructive. No way can I follow The Path while you are constantly Obstructing. The children and I are going where we can dedicate ourselves to Truth and Justice."

Andrea left this letter one day for her husband to find when he got home from work. By the time he found it, she was well on her way to somewhere unknown.

Andrea's husband, Paul, had been concerned for months about her involvement with The Path to Peace, a church that seemed to put more emphasis on getting along with The Father, as they called their pastor, than on anything else. Andrea's indifference to her job, her family's needs, and even her own well being had caused serious strain on the marriage. Paul had very mixed feelings when he found this note. Much as he loved Andrea, he did not know whether their marriage could have continued had she stayed. But he was not about to give up his two young children to the group. He set out to find them all.

No amount of information about staying connected and building trust will help much unless you are in touch with the cult member. What one group calls "disconnects" are not uncommon in cult involvement. Sometimes the member's disappearance is part of group policy, sometimes it's a punishment for your opposition, and sometimes it's the outcome of your interactions with the cult member. Often, as in Andrea's case, it's due to a combination of factors.

Whatever the cause, if a person you love has disappeared, your overriding first need is to find her. This chapter reviews the search process and discusses differences that may apply in cult cases. There are two parts to every search: the work of searching and preparing yourselves in the event you find the person. This chapter deals with the work of searching. The rest of the book will help you with the second task.

A search can be used against you. If, as is likely, the group learns about it, they will almost certainly present your activities as efforts to control the member and keep him from living his own life in his own way. They may tell the member that you are trying to kidnap and forcibly "deprogram" him, drawing vivid pictures of torture and starvation. Or they may ship the member out of the country to some remote and dangerous part of the world to make it harder to find him. On the other hand, the group cannot claim that you are indifferent to him or have disowned him. If you are looking for him, you care about him and he will know that.

Searching for a missing person is painful and difficult and does not always result in success. Don't despair, but don't believe any airy claims that if you just make the right moves, you will find the missing person. It's not necessarily so.

In the United States today, a standard search for a missing person assumes that the person earns income, pays rent, purchases goods on credit, holds a driver's license, and has been "misplaced," rather than actively sought to disappear. Much of this is not characteristic of cult members. They may work in exchange for board and room rather than drawing a salary and renting an apartment. They may be paid in cash or may hand their paychecks over to the group, rather than maintaining a bank account. They may have no credit cards and may not bother to renew their drivers' licenses. Nevertheless, this kind of conventional search is an appropriate starting point. Even a negative finding can be useful information.

The "how-to-find-someone" books and Web sites listed in the resource section at the end of this book spell out the search process in detail. These and other similar books are available in your public library and on the shelves of the larger bookstores. (Some of these publications may suggest activities of questionable legality. Even though you may be desperate, avoid such activities. The potential harm almost always outweighs the potential benefit.) Browse through one or more of these books to prepare yourself. For now, here is a quick summary of the basics:

Start by compiling a profile of the person you are looking for. The PRE-CULT IDENTITY CHART should have much of the information you need, which is:

- Name (present name and any others used, such as maiden name)
- Date and place of birth
- Social security number
- Last known address and telephone number

- Physical description, including any distinguishing marks, such as scars or false teeth
- Medical history, especially chronic conditions requiring medication or recurring problems like back pain that might lead the person to seek treatment
- Psychiatric or psychological history, if any
- Education and occupation (including last known employer)
- Marriage and/or divorce history
- Professional or occupational skills, licenses, qualifications
- Hobbies, interests, recreational activities

For clues as to where your loved may have gone, consult friends and family members to whom the member may have confided more than he did to you. Find out whether he dropped any useful hints or expressed any specific intentions (i.e., "Think of me next time you're shivering in the cold," or, "I'm going to be traveling a lot the next few months. I'll see you in the fall.")

Frequently, the recruit will write a note, as Andrea did, or call from a pay phone. This will persuade the police that the disappearance was "voluntary," and not a crime. It is not illegal to disappear (except when wanted by the authorities), so unless the recruit is under eighteen, do not expect the government to help with your search. Nor are the police likely to concern themselves with locating children who are the subject of a marital dispute (unless they have been taken in violation of a court order).

Once your profile is ready, you can do a great deal, either on your own or with the help of a professional investigator. (See *About the Group* and Appendix A for more information about this option.) You can write to the many government agencies with which your missing person might be in contact. For a fee, you can access certain large databases that track paper trails like credit data and drivers' records (although in some states, drivers' records are confidential and not available to the public). You can search under "Finding missing persons" on the Internet. Numerous resources are available there and elsewhere.

Don't be dismayed if this search comes up dry. The unusual circumstances of the cult's lifestyle may be the cause—or your missing person may not want to be found. Professional investigators readily acknowledge that it's much harder to find someone who is actively hiding.

In cult cases, there's an intermediate level that I call "passive" hiding. Cult members don't necessarily see themselves as "disappearing" when they set out on their travels. They fully intend to get in touch again sometime soon. They just keep putting it off. They know they're fine, so it doesn't occur to them that you are worrying. Thoughts of you are much less compelling than their focus on daily life in the group.

This unthinking kind of disappearance suggests that the recruit is not consciously rejecting contact with the outside world. Rather, she's lost touch with the realities of staying connected. In the fog of her new mindset, she has no sense of urgency about calling. "Tomorrow" never comes and she doesn't realize that it's been a week, a month, or longer since she sent that note.

There might also be a feeling that when she does call, the conversation might not be 100% pleasant, that you will carp and complain about her decision, about the unconventionality of her new lifestyle, and be generally what the group depicts as "negative" and "controlling." If she's not looking forward to it, and she's perfectly fine, why bother to call?

A person who is passively hiding might not bother to give you his new address, but doesn't really mind if you get it on your own. He doesn't write or call, but doesn't resent it if you do. If this is the situation, you have additional resources available:

- Call "Information" in the area where you think he lives and see if you can get a new phone number.

- If the recruit maintains an e-mail address, try sending e-mail.

- Send a letter to the old address, marked "Do not forward. Address correction requested." If there is a forwarding address, the post office will return your letter with the new address on it. (Don't ask them directly for a forwarding address. They won't give it.)

- A former landlord or rental agent may have an address where a refunded deposit is to be sent.

- A former employer may have a forwarding address for the W2.

In talking to people who may be able to give you this kind of information, be calm and matter of fact, as if the dog had eaten the slip of paper you wrote the address on. People will often respond readily to a routine inquiry, but may refuse if they sense anything out of the ordinary. Simply ask if there is a forwarding address and if so, what it is. Avoid lying, however, as a lie may come back to haunt you.

The group itself may be a resource. One father called the office of the cult in the town where his daughter had gone, asked for her phone number, and got it. Group publications and promotional materials (including Web pages) may list names of planners or participants in activities. Your loved one may be named, giving you a clue as to where she is and what she's doing.

Some groups are nomadic. They wander around with no fixed address and move whenever they feel in danger. When searching for members of groups like these or for someone who is actively hiding and does not want to be found, you need to think differently. One principle that professional investigators draw on in searching for "active" hiders is the idea that although people change their names and addresses, their personalities remain the same. Investigators recommend using occupational skills, hobbies, and recreational activities as a handle for pursuing these searches.

Suppose you are looking for Sam Sitwell, for instance. Sam has an accounting degree. He loves water-skiing and large dogs. He has changed his name. A professional investigator would look for an accountant who subscribes to the *Large Dog-Owners' News* and has a boat license or rents a slip at a marina. When the investigator finds such a person, he checks the date of birth. This may be a match.

This won't work in cult cases, of course, because the recruit has changed her personality, abandoning many things that used to be meaningful and enjoyable. But she is now closely following a *leader* who has quite a distinctive personality. If you've done your homework on the group, you have information about the leader. You probably know his name and—if he's changed it—his former name. You may have his birth date and social security number. You know something about his education, employment history, possible criminal record, and what geographic areas he frequents.

From the group's *Articles of Incorporation* and annual corporate reports, you may have the names of other group members. So you can look for the leader and the trustees. The cult leader may own property in his name, a family member's name, or a trustee's name. He may own a car or business or hold a credit card, and his whereabouts may be available through the classic databases that have no direct information about your loved one.

Furthermore, you can use information about the leader's personality and habits to look for him. Marshall Applewhite, leader of the Heaven's Gate group, sometimes lived with his followers and at other times, especially when they were migrating from place to place, lived nearby and occasionally dropped in to visit. Even though the group changed its ideology frequently and migrated across the United States, they left a trail of flyers and publicity about meetings. They had a Web page on the Internet. At least twice, the group settled, once in fortress-like quarters in Texas and once in the San Diego mansion where they died.

In the case of a small, nomadic group with no known base of operations, look for the leader's home town and family affiliations. Does he have an ex-wife and children (or other family members, such as siblings) somewhere? What part of the country does he know best? Does he have a preference for a particular fast-food chain? What brought the group to the city where your loved one was recruited? How long did the group stay there? What can you find out about their patterns of migration? How often and how far do they typically travel? Do they show seasonal or other predictable preferences for certain areas? You won't find the answers to all of these questions, but any information you glean may fit with some other piece, so it's worth asking every question you can think of.

Answers to these questions will come more easily if you can find a former member of the group you are looking for. Former members can help in many ways. They may know if the person has changed his name and/or occupation, what line of work the cult put him into, where they were likely to have sent him. They may even still have contacts within the group to help you try to track down the member or at least to confirm that he is somewhere with the group. They may have information about the group's usual ways of hiding people and some good ideas about how to find them.

The difficulty of finding former members varies, depending on the size and type of cult. If your loved one has joined one of the large, well-established groups whose practices have led disaffected former members to set up Web pages about their experiences, your search will be fairly easy. If the group is small and not well known, finding a former member can take a long time.

Check with the *bona fide* cult information and education organizations. (Be aware that the Cult Awareness Network's name and phone number has been taken over by owners connected with an organization that was strongly opposed to its activities. You are not likely to get useful information from that source. It has been rumored that they may pass on information they get from you to the group you are asking about. Of course, you may want this to happen.)

You may be able to contact former members through AFF (American Family Foundation), a cult research and education group listed in Appendix B at the end of this book, or through the Leo J. Ryan Education Foundation, a recently formed group in Bridgeport, Connecticut. Be sure you are connected to the Leo J. Ryan *Education* Foundation, as an opposing organization also calls itself the Leo J. Ryan Foundation. Some former affiliates of the original Cult Awareness Network are still active as independent cult information or cult education entities under different names.

When you are working with former members, keep in mind that groups change. Don't discount the value of information even if addresses and telephone numbers are no longer current or if their explanations of the group's ideology doesn't square with what you are learning. Focus on things like the leader's background and behavior patterns.

If you know where the group is, but cannot find your loved one, or if you have found and attempted unsuccessfully to contact her, consider an appeal to the group leaders. The larger, high profile cults are concerned about their public images. Several have made public statements saying they are for families and anxious to promote family peace in the aftermath of "conversions." If that's true, why would they object to forwarding a letter?

Although it's more burdensome to write, a written record of your contacts with the cult is also more of a potential embarrassment to the group. Their response or non-response is more provable and more evident.

Write to the highest authority in the cult, with copies to any other contacts you have in the group. State that you are concerned about your child's or spouse's well-being, have not heard from him or her for such-and-such length of time, and that you would appreciate the leader's help in re-establishing contact with your family member. If there were stormy scenes or a failed exit counseling preceding the disappearance, acknowledge that some very strong feelings have arisen between you, and state that you now are anxious for reconciliation.

Enclose a letter in an unsealed envelope for the cult to forward to your loved one. The letter should simply repeat what you have already told the cult leader: That you have not heard for a long time, that you are concerned, that (if appropriate) you realize you said and did things that upset her, but that you love her and miss her and want to get back in touch.

Many cults have regular meetings, classes, or other events that are open to the public. Find out when and where the cult's major gatherings take place. Your loved one or someone who knows her might be there and you might be able to develop at least a networking connection with her.

Think very carefully about how to do this. You, as a deeply engaged family member, might not be the best person to make this kind of contact. The cult member is likely to have a very negative mindset (perhaps growing out of experience, but probably also fostered by the cult) toward you. The shock of seeing you may cause her to scream, run, or otherwise remove herself without your having the chance to say one word. It will give the group an opportunity to engineer a confrontation and to accuse you of being sneaky and controlling. The member will be very susceptible to the group's suggestion that you had some sinister motive for appearing so suddenly and that she must run and hide somewhere else.

It is probably better to find a neutral person, or someone to whom the cult member is favorably inclined, to drop in on the event and network a bit. This must be a person—whether a family friend or a professional counselor or cult specialist—who is patient and calm and can get to the point in an unthreatening manner. It may take more than one visit. If you take this approach, plan very carefully in advance so that your intermediary can negotiate on your behalf.

If this is a group that engages in formal excommunication, by whatever name (i.e., "shunning," or "disconnecting"), don't even bother. All you would do is get someone in trouble.

If it is more of a situation where there has been major family friction with no formal order by the group to break contact, you may have a chance. The intermediary must convey that the member need fear no anger or unpleasantness and above all, no opposition to the group, from the contact and that your desire to see or speak with her is solely because you love her. You must be able to live up to that commitment.

A resource you might want to consider at some point, especially if you've been out of touch for a long time, is the Social Security Administration's Letter Forwarding Service. Social Security will send letters for missing persons to their home address or in care of their employers if the letter has important information that they think the missing person does not know and that the person would want to know. For details and to get the necessary form (Form SSA-L963), contact your local Social Security office. They will not tell you whether or not they found an address and forwarded the letter, but they will tell you if they cannot process the request or if they do not have a number for the person.

If your search is unsuccessful, renew it from time to time. Times change and people change. One failure does not mean permanent failure. Hard as it is to keep hoping, keep hoping.

Chapter Nine
The Family and Its Resources

The family is the traditional bastion of support and help in times of trouble. Cult involvement is no exception, and the family is the first place to look as you begin to assess your resources. What resources does the family have that you can use to help your loved one? What resources do you need? Can you get them? How? Are you weak in some important areas? Can you strengthen your resources in those areas?

The situation is unusual because the family member most in need of help—the cult member—is likely to deny needing help and to distance herself from the family. This can cause strains as other family members question the need for help or agree to the need but question the approach. Therefore, it's useful to make a systematic assessment of how the family works, who is able to help, who needs help, and what kind of help family members might be able and willing to provide.

Contacts between family members and with the cult member vary widely, but the strong emotional ties of family members to each other, the years of living together, and the shared heritage create a bond that is difficult, if not impossible, to sever. Tempers may rise, family quarrels may rage, and barriers may go up. Terrible, hurtful things may be said and done in moments of high passion or gross irresponsibility. A bond that should be loving and supporting may become a bond of anger or hatred—but the bond is there.

Bill, an ex-cult member whose family relations were troubled even before he joined the cult, once reminisced that "They did everything wrong— they told me I was crazy and the group was a bunch of nuts. Finally they told me to get out and leave them alone." When he walked away from the cult a few years later, Bill didn't turn to his family because he thought they would reject him again. Yet, when he finally made a tentative approach he was warmly welcomed. The family told him they would have welcomed him at any time if only he had called them. Bill himself, despite the family troubles, remembers that he often thought of his family and longed for a reconciliation.

Just as the PRE-CULT IDENTITY CHART helped sort out significant factors about your cult member, ABOUT THE FAMILY is a questionnaire to help you sort out important information about your own family. Most of the questions are open-ended, some calling for lengthy narrative answers. Write your answers on a separate piece of paper as you work your way through. It's a good idea to make several copies of this questionnaire and distribute them for other family members to respond to. The differences in perspective may provide valuable insights.

Because this is such a complex, sensitive area, consider working with a trained family counselor or therapist for one or two sessions while you develop this topic. Many therapists charge on a sliding scale, so don't assume the cost will be prohibitive. Be sure you are working with a properly licensed professional. It's desirable, but not essential that it be someone experienced with cult problems. (For more information on how to select a therapist or counselor, see Appendix A.) If you decide to start out on your own, be mindful of the possibility that you may need professional help if the stress levels rise uncomfortably.

Everything in your family's relationships may be wonderful, but that would mean you are a very unusual family. Most families have difficulties—people who are hard to get along with, financial pressures, health problems, divorces, tension between the generations, and so on.

Be honest about this and invite honesty from others, even if it includes unpleasant surprises. You may learn that others saw the Thanksgiving dinner you remember as a blissful family reunion as a tedious tribute to your authority. Perhaps the long hours you worked to pay for your son's orthodontics also bought you the label, "workaholic." You may have to acknowledge that charming Uncle Jamie is a compulsive gambler who time after time has sapped the family's financial resources to cover his illegal gambling debts. Honestly examining one's family may not be pleasant. But you must know the truth in order to defeat the lies of the cult.

When deciding just *who* is in the family, strive for a broad interpretation, with attention to the *role* a person plays as well as the blood relationship. For instance, Roy, a young college student, hardly knew his natural father, from whom his mother had been divorced for many years. Roy got along badly with his stepfather, but was quite close to his stepfather's brother, "Uncle Joe," who often visited and talked to him and was able to reason with him in moments of conflict.

Roy's family decided that, for purposes of cult involvement, all three men were "family." Roy's mother informed his natural father, whom she had hoped never to speak to again, about the disastrous situation.

Roy's father was concerned about his son's plight, educated himself about cults, and participated in the planning. He was able to reach out to Roy as an impartial well-wisher and establish a communications channel. Roy's stepfather frankly admitted his inability to get along with his stepson. He stayed quietly in the background, providing support and guidance to Roy's mother. Roy's old relationship with his "Uncle Joe" and his budding relationship with his father were both critical in convincing him to participate in exit counseling.

What about a family where you are one of eight siblings, five of whom live in distant cities and whom you seldom see or speak with? Don't write off the more distant siblings, but focus on the two you are close to. What if the cult-involved person had a serious romantic relationship, but was not married? It depends how you get along with him or her and how they feel about you and about the relationship. As you make these decisions, remember they're not cut in stone. If need be, you can change your mind as you work your way through ABOUT THE FAMILY.

ABOUT THE FAMILY starts with a series of questions about family dynamics. This tells you about the family's way of doing business and the family's power structure:

How are decisions made? Not all decisions are necessarily made the same way. One person may decide who does which household chores, another what kind of health coverage is best. Major decisions—such as whether or not to move—may be made by consensus, while day-to-day decisions may be made by individuals (or vice-versa). In some families, decisions are avoided as long as possible and are rarely articulated. They just happen. In other families, the family patriarch or matriarch makes decisions. In still other families, even the smallest decision, such as what movie to go to, cannot be made without extensive consultation among all family members. Knowing how your family makes decisions may help you get the support of the key decision-makers for your plan.

Is there a dominant person? Who? In some families, no one person is dominant. In other families there is competition for dominance. Sometimes there are conflicting opinions about who dominates. In one family, the wife viewed herself as the deputy and buffer between the children and their busy, irascible father and saw her husband as the one in charge. She was stunned to learn that everyone else, including her husband, viewed her as the one in charge.

Kevin, a young African-American was struggling with the problem of his wife Maria's involvement in a Bible group. Maria was not only spending all her time with the group, but was also threatening to divorce her husband if he did not join. Kevin loved his wife and wanted to save the marriage if he possibly could. Unfortunately, the key decision maker in his family was Grandmother, a powerful personality who had taken care of him while his mother worked, had made huge financial sacrifices to help him through college and who was deeply offended by Maria's new beliefs and bizarre behaviors. Grandmother thought that Kevin should cut his losses and get a divorce.

If Kevin persisted in trying to save his marriage, he would not only have to contend with all the difficulties of Maria's situation, he would be defying his beloved and powerful grandmother, causing much anger and grief. After thinking the matter through, Kevin decided his next step would be to talk to his great-uncle, Grandmother's adored younger brother. If the two of them agreed, they would have a much better chance of persuading Grandmother to be patient a while longer.

Dominance can change as the family changes, through illness, aging, distance, or even the cult involvement. Sometimes changes are sudden and dramatic. Sometimes they are so gradual you hardly notice them.

What are the family's strengths and weaknesses? Strengths are characteristics and resources that promote the family's well being; weaknesses are characteristics and needs that impede its well being. An open, trusting family atmosphere is a strength. So is financial stability. Family feuds and other stresses, such as unemployment, are weaknesses. Family strengths or weaknesses may be temporary, like the absence from home of a key family member, or lasting, like an ongoing chronic illness. Since any plan to help the cult member must build on family strengths and avoid or compensate for areas of weakness, the need to identify these characteristics is clear.

Would you describe your family as "close?" What does that mean to you? Some families are by custom and tradition more interdependent than others. "Closeness" is not a requirement for family cohesion and the opposite of "close" need not be "distant." "Close" can mean that family members are constantly telephoning each other to report on the day's events. It can mean that family members freely share and discuss their personal achievements, goals, problems, and activities. Or it can mean that family members are accustomed to unwanted intrusions on their privacy by another family member in a position of dominance.

"Closeness," in the sense of being able to work and plan with other family members in an open, trusting atmosphere, is a definite asset in dealing with cult situations. If you don't have it, you may want to think whether it's possible or desirable to bring it about.

Among the Senters, a fictional family, Henry and Amanda, the parents, have quarreled with cult member Terry. Henry is angry and wants to "write her off," but Amanda yearns for reconciliation. Henry and Amanda's formerly happy marriage is under stress because of their disagreements about how to deal with Terry

Ashley and Chelsea have become closer to each other since their sister's departure into the cult, but are angry with Terry because she has pressured them to join the group. Ashley, in law school, is somewhat removed from the family arena. Chelsea and her mother often quarrel over Chelsea's unconventional clothes and hairstyles. These conflicts bore Henry, who refuses to take sides.

Grandmother Irene Senter is concerned, but finds the whole thing very difficult to understand. Amanda's parents, the Wrights, are involved in the progress of Peter's incurable cancer and sometimes seem almost to resent her distraction from their problems as she worries about Terry.

Figure 1 shows how their relationships look on a chart. In this diagram, arrows indicate strained relationship, regular lines a good relationship. Thickness of the line indicates the relative intensity of the closeness or strain.

Figure 1
The Senter Family Relationship Chart

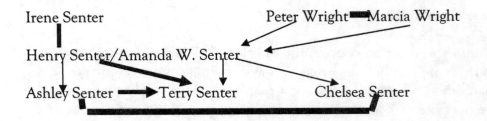

You can see how the cult involvement affects the whole family. It looks messy because it is messy. Terry's cult involvement has skewed everyone's life. Conflict exists where none existed before. Terry's sisters are pulled into the strain. Even her elderly grandparents are affected.

Who is close to whom and who is distant from whom and why? Try to chart this. On a piece of paper, make a family tree. Using a separate row for each generation, write the names of family members. Then draw lines to connect the members. Use a chain of "x's" to denote a bad relationship; dashes to denote a strained relationship; a single line to indicate a friendly, but not close relationship, and a thick or double line to indicate a close relationship. Describe relationships as they are now, not the way they were three months ago or the way you hope they will be six months from now

As you work through this exercise, don't feel obliged to connect everyone to everyone else. Use what you know and try to avoid jumping to conclusions. On the Senters' chart, it looks like practically no one is getting along with anyone else. Only the elderly grandparents and the two non-cult sisters are shown to have a close relationship. But the narrative adds important information. It shows that many of the strained relationships are due to the family's cult involvement. This kind of information can be a surprise to a family that thinks of itself as united and may point out the importance of working within the family to restore better relations as part of the overall plan for coping with the cult.

When a family member has a problem or conflict with another family member, what happens? Since families are made up of human beings, conflict is inevitable. Conflict in and of itself is neither good nor bad. What counts is how the family deals with it. In some families, confrontations are daily occurrences and disputes are settled at the tops of everyone's voice. This is fine if everyone is used to it and prepared for it. Other families consider conflict shameful or offensive and try to veil or ignore it. In some families, members routinely complain to the spouse or another relative of the person they have a problem with, but not to the person himself. Painful situations can arise when your remarks are passed on in distorted form to another family member.

How does this play out in the context of cult involvement? Is a family member who disagrees with your interpretation or plan likely to inform the cult member that you are concealing your disapproval? Is someone likely to disrupt family gatherings with ongoing grievances? Will your attempts to talk things over with family members be rebuffed? Will family members be able to reach out to you or the cult member when needed?

It's not unusual for a family member to deny responsibility for family quarrels.

> "I have no problem with Charlie," a family member once told me. "All he has to do is apologize."
>
> "Apologize for what?"
>
> "Apologize for the rotten things he said about me," which, it turned out, a third family member had conscientiously relayed to the offended person.
>
> "Would you like to make up with Charlie?"
>
> "I'll be happy to. All he has to do is apologize."
>
> "Would you be willing to call him up and ask him if he really said those things about you and, if so, ask him what he meant and give him the chance to explain?"
>
> "Are you kidding? I didn't start it and I'm not going to go crawling to him!"

Since this family was planning an exit counseling and wanted both Charlie and the angry cousin to be supportive, a peace-making effort had to happen first.

Some family members are likely to be in conflict with the cult member. If you are thinking about exit counseling, or even talking to or visiting the cult member, you need to know what feelings may pop up. Along with concern and a genuine wish to help, family members may feel anger at the recruit for taking up so much of their time and energy, or jealousy because she is taking up so much of yours. They may view her as a fool or weakling and emanate a kind of condescending pity. Even the "if-onlies," the guilty feelings about how you might have done things differently ("If only I'd gone to the movies with her that night, she never would have been in that coffeehouse"), can impair your judgment as you strive for a viable plan. Learn how family members signal conflict and what they do about it.

The section headed **"Recent family events"** asks for a review of family history from the start of cult involvement to the present. This will give you some perspective on changes that have taken place since the recruitment. If there was a death or other family upheaval at about that time, this may have some bearing on the situation. To the degree that the cult member has been out of touch with the family, this exercise can alert you to differences between what he remembers and the actual situation. It will also help you arrive at an overview of the family's current situation, just as you tried for an overview of the member's current situation.

You may find a variety of opinions among different family members about what has happened and how it has affected family members. Truth is complex. If you and your spouse have been tied up caring for an elderly parent or in-law, you may see this as act of love and caring. But perhaps your adult children, strained by trying to care for their pre-schoolers while holding down full-time jobs, feel short-changed because you are not available to help them. And the parent you are caring for may resent the loss of independence and the need to do things differently.

How has the family changed as a result of its cult problems? A cult problem impacts on the family as well as the cult member. Each case is different. There is no formula that will apply. A life has been derailed. A son, brother, or husband is suddenly not available. Children reject parents. Parents leave children. Spouses are abandoned. Cherished dreams and projects vanish. Often, abuse of trust is part of the picture. Money may be drained from a joint account. Clothing and furniture may be removed during the family's absence from the house. A period of weeks or months of systematic lying may be uncovered.

The family goes on—it has no choice—but changes are inevitable. Someone must to some extent assume necessary roles and functions of the lost person. One or many family members are expending time and energy learning about cults, trying to regain their balance, trying to help the cult recruit. While this is happening, other things are not being done. Try to identify and list these changes.

What, if anything, is bringing the family closer—or pushing family members apart? Include the cult involvement, but think about the family changes you listed at the beginning of the section and try to look at their overall impact on the family. Are you more united, more aware of each other and each other's needs? Or are you more scattered and less frequently in touch? What have all these changes meant?

Now, look at the family in crisis: **Review other crises that have occurred in the family. How did the family react? Are they reacting differently to the cult crisis?** Individuals react typically—though differently— in moments of crisis. Where one person collapses in tears, another might gobble up six ice cream sundaes and a third might indulge in a temper tantrum. Families also have habitual reactions. They may huddle together and conceal their stress from the outside world. They may turn to their church. They may focus on shielding one or more family members from suffering. If the family reaction to the cult crisis is different from the usual reaction, try to figure out why, whether the change is constructive or not, and whether it signifies growing strength or growing vulnerability in the family.

Family secrets are deliberate concealments of important family information. It's amazing how many families don't want even those who are closely affected to know certain things. An uncle or brother may have been incarcerated for a violent crime—and even close family members were told that he was working overseas. An adopted child may have been led to think she is a natural child. A family member who is often "ill" may be an alcoholic. A suicide may have been described as a natural or accidental death. Violence is often a very private family affair.

There are reasons to think very hard if you know of secrets like this: First, if the cult member knows about it, you can be sure that the cult knows about it and will use it against the cult member (and you, if you cause any "trouble"). Second, such secrets make it extremely hard for a family to work together effectively. If you don't know that Uncle Alec served a term for manslaughter, you may completely misinterpret your mother's anxiety that he not be provoked. A history of suicide in the cult member's family would lead you to give more weight to the depressive effects of cult involvement, and so on. Furthermore, such secrets are apt to be blurted out—either in anger or completely by accident—when tensions are high, as during an exit counseling.

Of all the ways of opening up a family secret, accidental discovery is the riskiest. To those not in the secret, it comes as shocking evidence of deception by those they trusted. For those who colluded in the secret, the feelings of shame and guilt that led to the concealment are unleashed. When added to the embarrassment of being caught in a deception, these feelings can completely overwhelm any efforts to do anything else.

This is not to advise that all family secrets be immediately—or ever—revealed to everyone. Simply take note that a secret of this sort is like a bomb. It is better either to disarm it or set it off in controlled conditions than to leave it lying around the house and hope no one will trip over it.

Now that you have done all this, how would you characterize the **family balance?** Is the family in danger of being overwhelmed by the cult catastrophe? Are there other family members whose difficulties have been neglected or obscured due to the cult crisis and who need help and attention? Is there a consensus within the family about the nature and seriousness of the cult situation? If not, is there something you can do to promote consensus?

Overall, **what are the family priorities?** Do you think they are appropriately balanced? If not, how can you achieve that balance? Keep this question in mind as you develop your plans in the next chapter.

Based on your review of the family, fill in the applicable parts of the FRIENDS AND FAMILY NETWORK, adding the names of any friends that come to mind at this stage. As always, make copies and set aside a blank copy so that you can redo and update the form as needed. Date the form so you will be able to place it in a chronological sequence as you continue to try new things.

The FRIENDS AND FAMILY NETWORK form asks you to list by name family members and others who might be helpful. After each name, the form lists eight different categories to help you determine objectively each person's potential to help. The response for some of the categories is a number and for some a letter. For the number categories, the more "1's" after a person's name, the better. For the letter categories, the first column asks you to identify possible problems that might interfere with the person's ability to help, so the fewer letters there, the better. The second letter answer column asks for ways in which the person is able to help, so the more letters there, the better.

This exercise is useful in confirming or confronting your instincts about people and clarifying why it would or would not be a good idea to involve them, as well as the ways in which they might help.

ABOUT THE FAMILY

A. Family dynamics

    1. How are decisions made?
    2. Is there a dominant person? Who?
    3. What are the family's strengths? Its weaknesses?
    4. Would you describe your family as "close?" What does that mean to you?
    5. Which family members are close to you? To each other? Why?
    6. Which family members aren't speaking to you? To each other? Why?
    7. When a family member has a problem or conflict with another family member, what happens?

B. Recent family events

    1. How has the family changed since the year before the cult member's recruitment?
        a. Marriages, births, divorces, deaths, employment, illnesses, moves, etc.
        b. How might these changes have affected the cult member?
        c. How have these changes affected others in the family?
    2. How has the family changed as a result of its cult problems?
        a. How might these changes have affected the cult member?
    3. What, if anything, is bringing the family closer?
    4. What, if anything, is pushing family members apart?

C. Think about other crises that have occurred in the family (Deaths, illnesses, divorces, unemployment, migrations, etc.)

    1. How did the family react?
    2. Are family members reacting differently to this crisis? If so, how do you account for the differences?

D. Family secrets - are there any? If so, is it time to do something about this? What?

F. Keeping the family balance

    1. Who else (besides the cult member) needs help and attention?
    2. How do other family members feel about the time and attention you are devoting to the cult member's situation?
    3. What is an appropriate balance of family priorities? How can you achieve that balance?

Friends and Family Network

Date _____

Name	Relationship to Member 1 = Close 2 = Not Close 3 = Distant		Relationship to Family 1 = Close 2 = Not Close 3 = Distant	Feeling about cult involvement 1 = great concern 2 = some concern 3 = no concern	Possible Problems (List all that apply) A = Physical Health B = Mental Health C = Behavioral D = Current Stress E = Family Conflict	Possible sources of support (list all that apply) A = Emotional B = Information C = Political, legal, media D = Skills E = Financial/material	Length of time known 1 = 5 yrs. + 2 = 1-5 yrs. 3 = < 1 yr.	Potential for personal involvement 1 = strong 2 = moderate 3 = possible 4 = unlikely
	Pre-cult	Present						
Household members								
Other family members								
Friends								

Chapter Ten
Resources: Possibilities and Limitations

The word "resource" is a broad descriptive term that means anything or anyone that might be helpful. A person who is close to you or the cult member or has a powerful influence on him or her for some other reason might be a resource. Equally, a person who has little knowledge of or emotional connection to the cult member might be a resource for a different purpose, such as exit counseling. Information, money, skills, access to the media, access to the cult member, or a particular household or personal item that is significant in the member's life are all resources. The most obvious resource—the family—has a chapter to itself. But do not overlook resources other than the family. Most of them are people and places you would naturally seek on your own, but skim the list just for the sake of thoroughness:

Friends

Friends are a wonderful source of both emotional and practical support. Include not just your friends, but also the cult recruit's friends in your survey of resources. Their information may be more accurate and more up-to-date than yours. They may have insightful ideas, and they are potential channels of communication should yours break down. The cult member may contact her—or even your—friends rather than talking to you directly. Friends have friends. Your friends may know someone who's great at searching the Internet for information, someone who has contacts in the media, or others who have other skills and contacts you can bring to bear on your situation.

People, Organizations, Books

People, organizations, books and other sources of legal, medical, political and other kinds of advice about specific problems may be very helpful. Do you think there may be a violation of the cult member's civil rights? Call the local American Civil Liberties Union. Do you think the cult is scamming the public with spurious products? Talk to the Better Business Bureau or your local government consumer protection agency. What are the health risks for a person going to India who doesn't believe in inoculations? Try the State Department. Don't know what organization or government agency might help with your problem? The reference librarian in your local public library can probably find out for you.

Don't stop at the first "no." Always ask the person who says he does not have the answer to suggest another place that might be better. Especially, don't let government agencies pass the buck too long. If you're dealing with a city government and don't get satisfactory answers, call the Mayor and talk to someone on his staff. State government? The governor. Federal government? Call your congressman for help. As a taxpayer, you're entitled to services. Elected officials pay attention to voters and will help you access services if you are having trouble.

DO state a specific question or problem you want help with, not a general complaint about a group. And be careful about using the word, "cult." It can be counterproductive when talking to organizations and government employees who are sensitive about appearing to take a position on a controversial group.

Media

Cults hate and fear adverse publicity, but seek and court the "Aren't they cute?" or the "Now here's something provocative!" sort of attention that is readily obtainable from talk shows hungry for daily sensations or magazines that have to fill a required number of pages each month.

The media are powerful, but treat them with caution—both as to what they tell you and what you tell them. Print and television reporters are always in a rush to "get a story," and may oversimplify or misstate information. If you choose to share information with reporters, be careful what you say and how you say it. A reporter will assume that everything you say is for publication unless you stipulate beforehand that it's "off the record." If possible, get the reporter to read to you before publishing exactly what is in the story about you and your family member, so that you have a chance to correct inaccuracies. You don't want to come across, for example, as a vindictive parent who just won't let his daughter grow up and be different.

Also, consider what the cult might do to punish you or your loved one if they think you are responsible for bad publicity—and be ready to pay the price. You may be in a position to do some trouble-shooting if you know in advance when a piece will be published and if you are in touch with the cult member. Contact him and inform him that you have talked with a reporter and tell him when and where the story will appear. If you've said negative things about the cult, acknowledge that—presumably it's no news to your cult member that you disagree with him about the group—and point out that you've said nothing you haven't already said to him. If you said neutral or positive things, point out that you used a balanced approach.

If you've turned to the press in a desperate attempt to find your family member and get in touch with her, as one family did, that will be clear from the story—and the publicity might pressure the group to cooperate, as it did for that family.

Although the media can sometimes be very helpful, be careful. You may pay a high price for getting the word out on the group that troubles you.

The Internet

The Internet can provide access within hours to amazing quantities of information. Feed the name of the group or its leader into one of the search engines and you'll come up not only with the group's Web page, if they have one, but a list of references to the group in other sources and, depending on the size and prominence of the group, postings of present and former members, bibliographies, and other materials in stunning profusion. You can get information about the town where the group is located, unfamiliar concepts or products identified in the group's materials, and many other questions that might arise as you pursue your research.

Caution is advisable, however. The content of the Internet is largely unpoliced. Information posted there may be absolutely correct, under- or over-stated, or outright false. Draw your own conclusions based on the source, the evidence offered in support of the assertions, and information you get from other sources. Just because it comes up on the computer doesn't mean it's true. See Appendix B for more on the Internet.

Ex-Members and Families of Former and Present Cult Members

For support and advice, there's nothing like talking to someone who's been there. People will share personally things you will never find in the newspaper or on the Internet, and you can share in return. Even if you can't find people who know firsthand about the particular group your loved one is in, it's a great comfort and relief to be where you don't have to explain it all. If you can find a local support group, try to attend. If you can get to a conference or other gathering of cult victims, try to go. As you share with and learn from others, though, remember that each case is unique. Don't let others pressure you into doing what worked for their family. And, conversely, don't refrain from doing something that is appropriate in your case but didn't work for their family.

Trained Counselors and Clergy

You are under emotional pressure, greater at some times than others, and your family life is disrupted. There is no road map on how to get out of this swamp and you may be coping with ethical or moral dilemmas. When you need balance, it's helpful to talk to an impartial but empathetic professional, bound to confidentiality and equipped with broad knowledge and experience of human behavior.

The caution here is that mental health professionals and clergy may not have much knowledge or information about cult involvement. If they are open-minded and willing to learn, they can be helpful very quickly. Unfortunately, many are not. It is important to interview a prospective counselor and to ask directly, "What do you know about the problems caused by destructive groups?" Appendix A has more on finding a trained counselor.

Exit Counseling/Thought Reform Consultation

Exit counseling, or what some prefer to call thought reform consultation, is an attempt led by one or more experts to engage the cult member in a dialogue that revives dormant thinking skills and explains how the manipulation took place. While the exit counselors attempt to impart information, family members supply emotional support and help persuade the member to stay and participate in what is often a lengthy, though entirely voluntary process. You will find much helpful information in Carol Giambalvo's *Exit Counseling: A Family Intervention*. Exit counseling is the best proactive answer developed so far for problems of cult involvement.

Exit counseling is also the process often misrepresented as "de-programming." In the 1970's, horrified parents sometimes retained "de-programmers" who kidnapped cult members, held them against their will, and harangued them about the evils of the group. There have even been allegations of abusive behavior by de-programmers. Some parents who saved their children by this method still endorse it, as do some former cult members who were rescued by deprogramming.

Exit counseling evolved as a less coercive, less confrontational approach, respecting the cult member more as a person and relying more on rational persuasion to help him or her find his way out of the cult. As the approach evolves, exit counselors are working more and more closely with families and family members are playing a far bigger part in the process. Exit counselors may also call themselves "thought reform consultants," a term which doesn't prejudge the goal of the intervention. See Appendix A for more on exit counseling and thought reform consultation.

However, exit counseling is feasible in only a minority of cases and when unsuccessful may sometimes backfire by increasing the cult member's alienation from the family. Is exit counseling likely to work in your particular situation? Here are some points to consider:

- Exit counseling works for many who already have doubts and hesitations, and who may, in effect, request it. If your cult member has indicated doubts about the group, or perhaps even moved away from the group or—as sometimes happens—been sent away from the group, exit counseling is a very promising option.

- Exit counseling is more likely to work for those who are strongly connected to you. Perhaps your cult member is young, still based in your home, and financially dependent on you, at least until recently. Or perhaps he or she has close ties and a warm and open relationship with you or other family members. If, on the other hand, you are dealing with a thirty-year old adult who has been on his own for ten years, living in another city and visiting now and then, the connection will be less compelling to him.

- Exit counseling is more likely to work for those whose allegiance to the group has been strained by abuse or obnoxious activities. Sometimes the group will make unpalatable demands—such as making a mother watch while her child is severely beaten—as a test of loyalty. While the member may conform for the moment, such experiences leave a lasting mark. Unfortunately, unless you know that things like this have happened, it is difficult to do more than guess on this point.

- Everyone, no matter how tight the group's grip, has "up" periods, when he feels happier and more connected to the group, and "down" periods, when he is unhappy and less connected to the group. You may not be able to predict the "down" times, but you can probably guess at, and avoid attempting an exit counseling during the "ups."

The highs come, as they do for all of us, at key group events or occasions—the visit of the Supreme Ruler, the celebration of his birthday (or wedding, etc.), the preparation for and enactment of the annual or biannual convention, revival, or jamboree.

If your cult member is in the United States, it's likely that an important group activity will be scheduled over Thanksgiving and at Christmas time, preventing members from visiting home at the times when the pull of the family is strong. Exit counseling is more likely to succeed if you can catch the cult member at a "down" time. You are handicapping yourself if you attempt an exit counseling in the weeks before and after a cult high spot.

- Exit counseling is unlikely to succeed if more than one cult member is present. This is one of the reasons cult members rarely visit on their own. If you are dealing with siblings or spouses, they will constantly reinforce each other unless you can devise a plan that allows you to work with one of them at a time.

Exit counseling is not a 100% solution. Estimates of success vary greatly, depending, for example, upon the specific group and the family's preparedness. Exit counselors report success rates of 80% or more for cult members who sit through at least three days of exit counseling. (This figure applies to those who haven't requested the counseling, but can be talked into it.) Many will not stay for three days and of those that do, a significant minority returns to the cult, anyway.

There is substantial downside risk in a failed exit counseling. Cults know about exit counseling and try to inoculate their members by suggesting that evil persons hired by their angry, controlling families might attempt to lure them with wicked lies away from the Truth to their doom. Members who resist exit counseling and return to the group may be welcomed as heroes and embellished tales of their ordeal and resistance may circulate widely. Their ties to the group are strengthened by the praise and recognition they receive. They may also be very angry with the family for enticing them into the situation. Painfully gained trust is lost and the relationship is set back as you strive to overcome the hurt and suspicion of the cult member.

On the other side of this complicated ledger, even though the member refuses to stay or ultimately returns to the group, exit counseling may plant a seed of doubt that forms the basis of an ultimate decision to leave.

Cost is a consideration. You will be obligated for the exit counselor's time and expenses even if the member walks out after a few minutes—or, at the last minute, doesn't come at all. Exit counseling costs may easily exceed $5,000. Exit counselors' fees vary widely and non-financial considerations, such as the exit counselor's age, personality, and knowledge of the group, are likely to dictate your choice. If we *knew* that exit counseling would work, the way we *know* an appendectomy will cure appendicitis, many of us would somehow find the money for it. But there is seldom any certainty about the probability of success in exit counseling.

Don't ignore the issue of how exit counseling might affect you. If one spouse is doubtful, but goes along, what will happen to your marriage if the exit counseling fails? If the exit counseling succeeds, but your loved one is extremely angry with you because of something that happened before or while she was in the cult, how will you react? If the exit counseling fails, and your loved one cuts off all communication with you, what will you do? Or, if you decide against trying an exit counseling, will you be haunted by the thought that you haven't done everything you possibly could to free your loved one from a terrible captivity?

While you should certainly consider the possibility of exit counseling, carefully weigh all the pros and cons, from questions of when, where, who, and why you think exit counseling would work, to the questions of what would happen if it fails and whether your money might better be spent on something else, such as counseling for you, other family members, or your loved one when/if he eventually leaves on his own. (Remember, most cult members who leave do so on their own.)

The pressure for haste may be enormous. But the mindset that you "must" do something before someone you love dearly enters into an ill-advised marriage, leaves for a prolonged stay in a remote or dangerous place, or throws away long years of professional training, can lead to precipitous action that reduces your chance of success.

Remember, you are combating months of indoctrination and the firm commitment of your loved one. Nor is this a question of "letting" or "not letting" something go forward. Unless the person you are concerned about is under 18, you have no authority over his or her actions. Try to weigh honestly the chances that a hasty intervention will succeed against the downside risk of increased estrangement and hostility if it fails. Try also to consider how your chances of success might increase or decrease if you wait longer and prepare better and/or if your loved one has a longer and perhaps more disillusioning experience in the group.

The Law

Lawsuits and other court-based activities, such as guardianships or Adult Protective Services may sometimes be helpful. You may want to consider bringing in the law. You may feel that you've been "robbed" of someone you love, that your family member has been deceived, defrauded, and cheated and that "there ought to be a law." Unfortunately, the law in areas related to undue influence and psychological coercion by cults is not well developed and the courts do not have clear standards. Additionally, courts are reluctant to intervene where First Amendment rights to freedom of speech and freedom of religion appear threatened. The Commission on Mental and Physical Disability Law of the American Bar Association has published a study on this subject, *Cults in American Society: A Legal Analysis of Undue Influence, Fraud and Misrepresentation.* (See Appendix B.)

Not only is there small chance of success through legal action, there are many negative possibilities. Once a matter is in the hands of the court, it is out of your control. All sorts of private affairs may be opened up through depositions and documents you are required to surrender to the other side, and you may endure a mauling on the witness stand. Costs are uncontrollable—your attorney, for example, will have to do what the court orders, however long it takes—and you cannot stop when you have used up a budgeted sum. Time is uncontrollable. Courts move in unpredictable patterns and even a matter that is argued in a timely manner may sit for years on the judge's desk, waiting for decision.

Furthermore, the group is likely to portray you as traitorous, devilish, and dangerous to the cult member. If you should happen to win, it is possible you will face greatly increased hostility on the part of the cult member (unless he or she was ready to leave the group or enlightened as to its deception during the course of the proceedings).

Nevertheless, do not hesitate to seek legal advice if you want to. A skilled attorney may negotiate in arenas other than the courtroom and dispassionate, professional advice on legal aspects of the situation may prove valuable.

A different kind of involvement with the law arises if, in the course of your investigation, you come across information about crimes committed or about to be committed by the group. Sharing this evidence with the appropriate authorities, such as the police or the District Attorney, may be imperative, as in situations where someone's life is at stake.

Pressure on the Group

Another possibility some families are drawn to is the idea of getting the group to expel the member, through bribery, making oneself a nuisance to the group, or other method. This is a highly questionable strategy for two very important reasons:

First, the member is likely to find out how he or she came to be expelled. You will stand convicted of the same kind of deception and manipulation you are accusing the group of engaging in. Worse, the cult member will hold you responsible for his expulsion from "paradise." You may in time succeed in restoring his thinking processes and he may even come to agree with you about the group. But how will you repair the damage done in his eyes to your integrity?

Second, be aware that clinical experience indicates that people expelled from cults are more likely to be seriously depressed, even suicidal, than those who leave of their own volition. You may be endangering your loved one's life.

Illegal and Unethical Behaviors

These are really two different categories, but both are ill-advised and undesirable possibilities. Twenty-five years ago, when parents first began trying to cope with cults' recruitment of their college-aged offspring, kidnapping/deprogramming seemed to many to be a reasonable solution. Some middle-aged adults today will tell you they are grateful to their parents for having them kidnapped. Without passing judgment on families in circumstances we cannot know, we do know that illegal activities may result in a jail sentence, loss of your right to vote, physical violence that harms individuals, and financial and professional ruin. Don't break the law. In addition to the consequences if you are caught, lawbreaking involves other, major negative consequences. See the next chapter for details if you are feeling tempted.

Unethical behavior may also cause harm. Behavior that violates your integrity, such as guaranteeing that you will not attempt an exit counseling when you are actually planning one, may come back to haunt you. Stating publicly that the cult leader is a wonderful man when in fact you think otherwise may serve your own needs, but may help mislead others. A nationally famous Hollywood figure issued warm statements of open mindedness and support for his son's group, but later repudiated his remarks after the son left. How many families were lulled into acceptance by this endorsement?

This is not to say all subterfuge is unethical. If you want to stay in communication with the cult member, you will probably have to project complacency and calm that you really do not feel. You may plan to attempt an exit counseling at the end of a week's vacation together without mentioning that part of the plan to the cult member—simply because you would never get her home if she knew of the plan.

Dilemmas may arise and you may find yourself struggling with questions of legal and ethical behavior. If you learn the cult is smuggling drugs into the country, are you morally or legally required to report it? Questions like these may call for legal research, thoughtful deliberation and perhaps counseling with your minister or other trained counselor.

Use your experience, balance out the pros and cons as best you can, take your time, and don't be stampeded into hasty decisions. You are in a difficult, delicate situation, in unmapped territory, and your compass may be spinning. You and the cult member must live with your decisions afterwards, so move thoughtfully and carefully.

Be honest about limitations. Some common limitations are:

- **Financial limitations**. Perhaps you can afford an exit counseling, but only at the cost of a large chunk of your retirement funds. Perhaps you can afford to pay high-priced, last minute plane fares for a visit to the cult member, but only if you give up a long-planned trip to a family wedding. Perhaps your savings are already depleted by some other emergency and you need to rebuild your reserves before spending any more. These are real and difficult dilemmas and you must make thoughtful, careful decisions.

- **Practicality.** You may be absolutely certain that if your daughter knew how sick her mother was, she would come home—but if you can't get that information to her, you can't build a plan based on this premise.

- **Need for the cooperation of critical parties.** Marriages have split over disagreements about cult problems in the family. Cult members' friends or other family members may secretly feel the parents are making too much of their friends' involvement. If, just as your exit counseling gets rolling, a skeptical brother is going to pop into the room and ask, "Well, is she out yet?" your problems will only be worse.

- **Allocation of time and energy.** Considering all the other things you have to do, such as earning a living and caring for other members of the family, can you and the others involved realistically meet the demands of your plan? If you want to visit for a week every third month, for example, be sure you can really take the time off work before you commit to doing it.

It is better to acknowledge limitations and set up a plan that you can realistically carry out than to set yourself up for failure by attempting something that is beyond your reach. This is not to discourage you from imagining possibilities, but to help you balance your wishes and your capabilities.

Once you have some general ideas about your resources and your limitations, you are ready to work on a strategic plan.

Chapter Eleven
Developing A Strategic Plan

People leave cults for many reasons.

One person told me the following story: He had always longed for a dog, but never had one. Family relations were badly strained when he was involved with the cult, but he did occasionally see family members. One day a family member, simply trying to express her love and retain the connection, unexpectedly gave him a puppy. The puppy took up a lot of the cult member's time and attention. Puppies need to be fed regularly. They need to be walked, trained, washed, and loved. He took good care of the puppy, but this interfered with the group's demands and they ordered him to get rid of the dog. But he had longed for a dog all his life. Instead of giving away the dog, he left the group.

Of course, this wasn't the only cause of his departure—he was already questioning many things about the group—but it certainly helped. This story underlines two very important points:

- **Mind bending is never 100%.** The little boy who longed for a dog grew into a young man who still longed for a dog. Nothing in the cult experience changed that yearning. There are such places in everyone. Try to find them.

- **The agenda of the group will inevitably clash with the individual's needs.** This will probably happen in both lesser and greater matters, and more than once. In the "honeymoon" stage, when the member is thrilled to be associated with such wonderful people, suppression of one's own needs may pass almost unnoticed, or may be framed as a test of the new member's dedication—a sacrifice on the altar of greatness. Later on, the differences may become far more significant to the member and indeed, crucial. Mothers tell of leaving groups because they could no longer bear to see their children beaten, for example.

Begin your planning with a review of the MEMBER'S PRESENT SITUATION, revised and updated as well as you can. As you organize your resources and identify your options, keep in mind the factors that will make it easier and more attractive for the member to leave than to stay.

The purpose of the STRATEGIC PLANNING WORKSHEET is to help you organize and evaluate the ideas and information collected as you worked through your assessments. As with all these forms, make several copies and keep a blank sheet handy so you can make more if you need them. Be sure to date each one.

Before you begin to work with the form, stretch your creativity with some serious brainstorming. Brainstorming is an easy way to encourage original thinking, expand options, and generate possible solutions to a problem. Brainstorming can be a one-man operation or a group exercise. It can happen at any time or place. Some people do their best brainstorming in the shower (although one must remember to write ideas down later) or while stuck in traffic. Others like to sit comfortably in an easy chair with soft music in the background. If you have a group, with two, three, or more participants working together, the process is still the same.

Start by coming up with ideas about what you can do to help your family member (or yourselves). Write every suggestion down, no matter how silly or impossible it sounds. Don't use the WORKSHEET for this. An ordinary piece of paper is better. Collect as many ideas as you can without appraising, criticizing, or commenting on them in any way, since the goal is to be open and receptive to new ideas. If participants are worrying about what others will think of their ideas, they may be hesitant to share them.

Ideas can be as large as "exit counseling," or as small as "send a postcard." A brainstorming session may start slowly, with few ideas being offered. Keep at it until you have at least a dozen, but hopefully, dozens. Of course you can add more ideas that pop up as you evaluate those already suggested. That's part of the process.

Once you have listed all the ideas you can think of, begin to evaluate and organize them. The first step is to eliminate proposals that are illegal. There may be discussion about this, with some arguing that so much is at stake that such behavior is justified. But consider the disadvantages:

1.   Loss of integrity. Kidnapping or physically detaining a person against his or her will, for instance, is illegal. How can you argue

that it is wrong for the group to break the law if you have broken it yourself?

2.   Loss of trust. It is harder to convince a person who has been physically coerced that you did it out of love or concern. This feels like an attack, not like a loving act, and is not likely to improve the chances that someone will respond openly or positively to the information you convey.

3.   Confirmation of the cult's negative portrayal of the outside world as hostile and dangerous. Cults use lurid tales of kidnappings and deprogrammings derived from early anti-cult history as a bugaboo to frighten members and increase their fear and worry about visits with family members.

4.   Blackmail or other damage from those who know what happened. Seldom can such illegal activities be carried out without outside assistance. When committing an illegal act, you may find yourself involved with people who have far fewer scruples than you about breaking the law or profiting from the consequences. The cult member himself, if he can free himself, may later bring charges especially if he returns to the group.

5.   Unintended harm. A person struggling with a kidnapper could suffer or inflict severe physical damage.

6.   Legal penalties.

7.   Failure - success is never guaranteed ~ leaving you still exposed to the above risks. Experience and some research suggest that deprogramming, even disregarding the legal and ethical disadvantages is not as effective as voluntary interventions. An early study (Langone, 1984, cited in Langone, 1993) found that the cult member returned to the cult in approximately one-third of deprogrammings. Nearly 10% of the cases resulted in lawsuits.

Even if you have reason to believe someone is in imminent danger, acting outside the law is highly risky. Notify the authorities, rather than stepping in personally. This also helps you to distinguish between your fears of danger and the actual evidence of danger. It is terribly hard to see someone you love going off to the jungles of Brazil or a peak in the Himalayas or some other remote and dangerous place. But the law does not presently allow you to step in and prevent this. Hard as it may be to see it happen, you are better off using your time and energy to improve communications than engaging in risky plots.

Next, review "impossible" ideas, like "Go back to last December and start over." Obviously, you can't go back to last December, but consider what happened last December and if it is possible to re-build the relationship to where it was and how you might go about it. Then try re-phrasing the idea so that it is a possibility. For the time being, keep it on your list.

Once you have eliminated the illegal and the impossible, begin to fill in the STRATEGIC PLANNING WORKSHEET. Step (1) is to list in the first column, "Idea," each helpful suggestion that family and friends can legally and ethically do.

As you go down the list, tackle any ethical considerations that arise and discuss them immediately, even though you may not come to a conclusion on the spot. Ethics—the question of the morality of an activity or behavior—is a far more complex and personal issue than legality. Activities or behaviors that you do not generally engage in may well be acceptable in dealing with cult involvement. "All's fair in love and war," the old saying goes, and cult problems are both. Is it unethical to pretend neutrality about your loved one's involvement in a group you believe is harmful? Is it unethical to engage your loved one in exit counseling by saying, "Here is a person who has a lot of information about your group and would like to talk to you about it," even though it doesn't fully reveal your agenda?

Most people would find those stratagems perfectly acceptable, given the facts of the situation. But what about hiring someone to infiltrate the group and "make friends" with your family member—in effect, a spy? What about anonymously accusing members of the group (or even your own family member) of child or drug abuse in order to check out your suspicions or simply to unsettle the group? Think things through carefully as you go and you will reject many such ideas on ethical grounds.

After you have entered the ideas one by one in the "Idea " column, fill out as many of the other columns as you can for each idea. For instance, the idea may be "Try to communicate by e-mail." Don't let that idea die even if you don't have a computer and don't understand e-mail. Look at the next column, "What family and friends can do." Can someone else help you with access and training? Probably. Do you know someone who has a computer with access to the Internet? Write their name (or names) under "Key family and/or friends." Under "Requirements for success," you would probably write something like, "Learn computer skills, use of computer, get e-mail address, get his e-mail address." "Downside risk" might be "more angry exchanges, group abuses e-mail address and sends a lot of spam," or other things, depending on the type of group and your relationship with the cult member.

Don't hesitate to consider an idea that seems counter to conventional wisdom. There may be reasons it would work for you.

One family, for instance, repeatedly insisted to their cult-involved son that the theology of his group was wrong and they cited an expert on cults as their source. They even gave their son the expert's phone number and said, "If you don't believe us, talk to him."

After many arguments, the son one day said, "Give me that number again. I'm going to talk to him just to prove you're wrong." He actually did call the number and, after conversations with the expert, he left the group.

Don't worry if you can't fill in all the columns right away. As you go back over your list, you'll find yourself having more ideas. Filling out all the columns for each item might be a matter of days or weeks, and of course you might never complete some entries. But when you've gone over the list once or twice and done what you can for the moment, move on to the next step.

Step (2) tells you to identify three categories of items: Those that are easiest, those that are the most important, and those that must be done first (before other things can be done). It's a good idea to mark these ideas in the margin: "E" for "easy," "I" for "important" and "F" for "first." If there are other key planners involved in the process, make this a joint undertaking and try to reach a consensus on your designations. This is a good opportunity for serious discussion of the pros and cons of the various items. You may be lucky and find that one or more items meet all three criteria.

You can deal with Step (3)—eliminating ideas that are impractical or unacceptably risky—anywhere along the way as you organize the ideas on your list, or as a separate exercise after you finish filling out all the columns. A rough way to measure risk is to ask:

- What is the best possible thing that could happen as a result of trying this?
- What is the worst? Am I prepared to live with that if it happens?
- What is the most likely outcome?

Assessing the practicality of an idea involves three additional questions:

- What resources are needed to do this?
- Do we have these resources or have access to them?
- Provided we have the resources, is the likely outcome, or even the best outcome, worth the cost in time, money, and energy?

Be realistic when you assess the practicality of an idea, especially about your own resources. It can be painful to reject an otherwise good idea because it will cost you too much time away from your job, for instance, but on balance, you and everyone else are probably better off if you stay employed. Decisions like this may be very difficult to make, but if you think about the pros and cons and discuss them ahead of time, you will have a better basis when the time comes to decide. Another limitation may be the needs of other family members. After meeting the immediate needs of those around you, you may not have much time or energy to devote to someone who is far away and difficult to reach. It then becomes doubly important to make the best use of the time and energy you do have to spend on the cult member.

You will probably find that it is easy to assess the practicality or risk of some ideas and difficult for others. If you have doubts, or think it's a close call, leave the idea on the list, but reserve any action until you can resolve the doubts.

Step (4), organizing and prioritizing your activities, gives shape to your plan. Hopefully, your painstaking review will have helped you open up some new possibilities. You should now have a good idea of what you can do. You will know what is easy and what is hard or impractical. You will know if some things must be done in sequence and what steps come first. You will also have a much clearer idea of what you cannot do. You may even find that you have already done everything you can and that you can only go on doing what you're doing now. There is a sort of negative comfort in knowing this. Hard as it is to admit how little you can do to change this miserable situation, it is harder still if you keep thinking that you ought to be doing more.

Use the plan as a guide, not as a blueprint. Flexibility is critical. For instance, suppose part of the plan is sending cookies (which, last time you checked, was OK). The cult member may react, "Why'd you send cookies? Don't you know sugar is bad *chi?*"

Obviously, something has changed. Use the opportunity. Find out why sugar is now bad *chi* and ask what it is OK to send. Either there must be something or the member will have to say, at least to herself, "You are not allowed to send me anything."

Or suppose, on a grander scale, you have very patiently worked out a plan for a vacation together, and the member cancels at the last minute or, as sometimes happens, demands to bring a companion with her (at your expense). How will you handle these dilemmas?

Another aspect of flexibility is readiness to take advantage of opportunities. Some opportunities are planned and may be the result of much effort, such as a member's visit home. Others may be totally unexpected. Try not to miss these moments.

Mark Laxer, a former member of a New Age computer group, tells in his book, *Take me for a Ride,* how, after many doubts and difficulties, he left the group. He drove across the continent to New Hampshire and called his family, who flew from New York to Boston to have dinner with him. But he could not bring himself to tell them he had left the group. After several days of aimless wandering, during which he missed his friends from the group more and more, he drove back to the group, where he remained for another year. Could his family have done something that would have helped him? Maybe yes, maybe no. How would you prepare yourself—and the member—for a similar outreach?

If you sense a change, either that the cult member is retreating deeper into the group, or that she is finding it less satisfying than formerly, don't jump to conclusions. Assess the situation. Is her sudden interest in returning your phone calls a signal that she's more interested in hearing from you now? Is she softening you up to prepare you for some demand on behalf of the group? Is there more freedom to communicate because she's about to vanish and the group does not want you to report her missing? Ask yourself what information you need to understand the situation. Where can you get this information?

Chances are that no matter how well you have prepared, you will run into surprises. Remember that it's always all right to express your confusion and take some time to reflect.

The last part of a good plan is evaluation. As you organize your ideas, ask yourself if there is any way to know if something is working. Does the idea meet one or more of the basic criteria at the beginning of this book? Does it increase your (or the cult member's) knowledge, improve communications, or build trust? How? How might you know if the idea is not working?

You may have great difficulty evaluating the success of your ideas because you cannot count on reliable feedback from your loved one. She may state that she loves the beautiful new sweater, while in fact the leader's girl friend has taken possession of it. She may enter cheerfully into plans for a family reunion with no intention at all of attending it. On the other hand, she may be completely disaffected from the group, but unwilling to share that information with you. Don't blame yourself unduly, therefore, for missing signals or lost opportunities. If you are keeping in touch and making opportunities for yourselves to show your love and commitment, you are doing well.

Finally, don't expect any miracles. Miracles are wonderful when they happen, but they don't happen often. It's easy to adjust your plan if things go better than expected, so you need not spend much time worrying about this eventuality. Much more likely is a real-life, indeterminate, shades-of-gray, this-is-good-and-this-is-bad situation where things work out at less than their optimum but more than their minimum possibility. Be patient. Be hopeful. Endure.

STRATEGIC PLANNING WORKSHEET

Date _____

(1) List the things family and friends can legally and ethically do that will help
(2) Identify: the *easiest* things to do, the *most important* things to do, and those things that must be done *first*.
(3) Eliminate items that are impractical or unacceptably risky.
(4) Organize and prioritize your activities. Keep the plans flexible. Review and update them periodically.

Idea	What family & friends can do	Key family and/or friends	Requirements for success (e.g., time, money, travel)	Downside risk

Chapter Twelve
Returning

A prominent thought reform consultant tells the following story: A family seeking to help a young man out of the cult conscientiously went through a long, elaborate preparation process, followed by a long-drawn-out, but ultimately successful exit counseling. After several days of intense discussion and soul-searching, the young man announced, "I think I should leave the group." The family was thrilled.

Then came reality. Where should he go? What should he do? Nobody in the family had a readily available room where he could stay for an unlimited time until he was able to support himself. The family collectively didn't have or wasn't willing to put up the money for him to live in a place of his own until he got himself back together and found a job. While in the cult, he had antagonized everyone, and despite their understanding of why this had happened, there were lasting consequences. As they discussed what to do, it began to sink in that this young man was not really wanted in his family. The upshot was ironic, but logical. He went back to the cult.

Or consider this: A young woman left the group of which she had been a member for two or three years. When she sought help in learning about cults and cult involvement, she made a condition that her family not be informed that she had left. "After the way they behaved," she said, "they'll be the last to know I'm out!"

In cases of cult involvement, the exit is not the end. Should you have the connection, perseverance, and good fortune to see your loved one leave the group, a new set of issues immediately arises. Where to go? What to do?

Life will not go back in time to pre-cult days. The person who comes out of the cult will be different from the person who went in. He will have different skills, knowledge, and interests from his former self. A scholarly, introverted person may have learned in the group to manage a large retail enterprise. Or a diffident young social worker may emerge from the cult a computer programmer. Some of these changes, or some part of them, may stick.

The former cult member will carry a large bundle of experience, both good and bad, that he does not share with his family and pre-cult friends—and they will have a large bundle of experience not shared with him. There will be uneasiness on all sides, the recollection of stress and strain and, perhaps, behavior that all regret.

The family will wonder, "Is he really out? What if he goes off on his own? Will he go back? " If the new ex-member seems sad or disoriented, they may be concerned for his safety or his continued independence. They may wonder. "Will the next con man he runs into recruit him into something else?" They may, like the family above, find it impossible to overlook the hurt and destruction of the cult years when actually confronted with the need to take a chance now.

The ex-member will be bewildered and perhaps sad. He will not know whom to trust, where to go. He may have trouble making decisions, both large and small. He will probably worry about the friends left behind in the cult, especially those whom he recruited, and wonder how he can get to them, to help them see what a scam it is and leave. He may feel ashamed of things he did while in the group. He may have serious health problems. He may be out of touch with much of the world. Long-held beliefs, such as "It is wicked to eat meat," may continue to affect him even though the basis for accepting them is gone, so the ex-member finds it strange and repellent to enter a house or a restaurant full of meat smells. Perhaps most critically, he has learned and acknowledged that the great ideal to which he gave his all is a sham.

Members of the group may attempt to re-claim him, phoning, running into him in the supermarket, showing him the friendly, loving front that first attracted him—or perhaps threatening or even blackmailing him with the private information he had shared while a member. One group sometimes tries to discredit the exit counseling process, calling thought reform consultants, "hired guns," as if there were something discreditable about experts being paid for their expertise.

Recovery is not the subject of this book, but awareness of recovery issues must be part of every plan. Options for immediate action are essential. Think about this even as you work to bring about the exit.

Be ready to present a few possibilities to your loved one when the moment comes, and to help her think things through and reach some basic decisions. Will you take the newly exited person back into your home? Will he or she want to move in with you? Are you prepared to subsidize her for perhaps months until she is able to work and can find a job? Is there a way to get needed medical or mental health care for someone who has no insurance and has not been your dependent?

What if she's out, but like the young woman above, still doesn't want you in her life? How will you even know?

After the immediate problems, the ex-member may have to deal with longer-range problems, some of which may be immense: dissolution of a group-arranged marriage, custody of children left in the group, severe medical or mental health conditions, to name a few. Remember that your goal from the beginning has been to restore this person's autonomy, his or her sense of independence. These are problems for the ex-member to deal with. If she seeks your advice and help, do what you can to help, but don't take over the problem. You are not ultimately responsible for the decisions that must be made.

Dealing with cult involvement strains our human capabilities. It demands patience, study, caution, ingenuity, self-discipline, reflective thinking, and occasional daring. It requires bearing pain, combating our instincts, controlling our impulses, and always hoping. All these difficulties are compounded by the lack of public acknowledgment that there can be such problems and by the tendency of friends and the legal and mental health professions to regard worried family and friends as closed-minded or over-controlling.

Nevertheless, our knowledge and understanding have advanced considerably. Between the great resource of the Internet and the willingness of more and more former cult members to share their experiences, untold sources of information have opened up. Although scientific research is proceeding somewhat more slowly than a snail's pace, this book applies knowledge of human behavior to a wealth of information about specific experiences. Hopefully your understanding has broadened and you have acquired new tools to help you cope.

Appendix A
Finding Expert Help

Finding a Therapist or Counselor

People from several different disciplines and professions serve as qualified counselors. Psychiatrists, psychologists, clinical social workers, and, in some states, professional counselors, are all recognized mental health professionals. The most significant difference among these professions is that psychiatrists are medical doctors who specialize in mental health. Psychiatrists tend to do less counseling and more management of medications. A counselor from one of the other mental health disciplines may refer you or a loved one to a psychiatrist if she thinks medication might be in order. A psychiatrist might make a recommendation as to medication and refer you on to a social worker for counseling. Additionally, many schools of theology provide formal training in counseling. If you prefer to look to your church, your minister, priest, or rabbi may be able to refer you to a qualified pastoral counselor.

Reputable practitioners in any of these disciplines should be fully credentialed and licensed by their respective professional boards in the state where they practice. It is important to work with a licensed practitioner. Not only does a license guarantee at least a minimal level of professional training, it also provides a route for complaints (to the state licensing authority) should any problems arise. You need not rely on an individual's assertion that he or she is licensed. Licenses, which cannot be obtained without appropriate credentials, should be on display in the counselor's office. Do not hesitate to ask anything you want to know about a prospective counselor's training and credentials.

Ultimately, the professional affiliation of a prospective therapist or counselor is less important than his or her ability to help you. Shop for a therapist or counselor as you would for a doctor, a lawyer, or any other specialist to whom you will be entrusting private, sensitive information and whose recommendations might have a critical impact on your life.

Before you commit to working with a counselor, ask what kind of experience he or she has had with problems of cult involvement. Unfortunately, few counselors do have this experience, so you may have to work with someone who is less than optimally qualified. However, an otherwise qualified counselor who is willing to equip herself by reading a couple of books and learning from and with you can be quite helpful. Be sure that any prospective counselor has at least an open mind on the subject. There is no point trying to work with someone who doesn't believe that destructive cults exist or who has some other theoretical objection to your view of the matter. For example, the marriage counselor whose basic premise is that the blame is always spread about evenly between both spouses will not be helpful when a spouse is lost in a cult. Similarly, the family therapist who insists that problems parents have with their college-aged children are intrinsically "separation-individuation" problems will not be able to work effectively in cult situations.

Decide what your principal concerns are. You might need short-term, immediate assistance just to help you get yourself together. You might have decided to address a long-standing problem, such as drinking, to improve your ability to cope with this new dilemma. You probably can, and should, find counselors with experience in those areas. If you want to work intensively toward planning an intervention with the cult member, you will need someone who at least is willing to work with an expert on cults. Ask about the prospective counselor's experience and qualifications. Counselors, like other professionals, tend to specialize. Few, if any, are equipped to deal with all problems. Ethical professionals will tell you plainly if they do not think they can help with your problem.

Fees are another topic to discuss in advance. Fees vary widely. Pastoral counseling may be available without charge. Your health insurance may cover some or all of the costs. Some counselors charge on a sliding scale. Most mental health professionals charge by the hour and some will tell you at the end of the first or second session approximately how many sessions they think you will need.

How to find the right counselor for you? Ask around. A referral from a friend or colleague who has been helped by a therapist, or from someone you know who has suffered from cults, is one of the best ways to find competent help. Most clergymen can recommend counselors, as can school guidance counselors or student affairs offices of colleges and universities. State and local units of professional societies may have referral services. You may also have access to a local social service or mental health agency. AFF (American Family Foundation) lists some professionals with expertise in cults on its Web site, www.culticstudies.org.

In addition to competence, availability, and agreement on a fee, it is very important that you feel comfortable with your therapist. If you do not feel comfortable with people who dye their hair purple, do not work with a therapist who dyes her hair purple. Ask about the therapist's methods of treatment. If you do not want to sit on a pillow on the floor, do not work with a therapist who has clients sit on pillows on the floor. Be aware that no reputable therapy calls for a client to scream, roll on the floor, disrobe, or engage in other bizarre behaviors. Avoid therapies that are not rationally or scientifically supported or that require you to make great leaps in faith to go along with them. Even after you have begun work with a therapist, feel free to end the relationship if you begin to feel uncomfortable or if you are not making progress toward your goals.

Finding an Investigator

If you are planning to retain an investigator, you will probably want to find someone who works in the city where the group's headquarters are located, or where your loved one lives. It is always more difficult to make a decision about someone you haven't met personally. Although most of the suggestions in this section are oriented toward long-distance work, they should also be helpful if you are looking for an investigator in your own area.

Like mental health professionals, reputable private investigators have licenses. And, as with mental health professionals, the possession of a license assures a modicum of training and provides an address for complaints if necessary.

Investigators' backgrounds and experience vary widely, as do their clientele and areas of specialty. Some private investigators specialize in background checks of individuals. Others may focus on store security, an area of expertise less likely to be helpful to you.

Some investigators subscribe to key databases and can retrieve information about property ownership, tax liens, and so forth, from computers in their own offices. Others must go out to public places, at your expense, to access databases. Many investigators are former police detectives, FBI agents, or other former law-enforcement officials and have good access to their former agencies. Many have specialized skills in law, accounting, or criminal justice.

Interview at least two and preferably more investigators by phone before choosing one. Decide ahead of time what you want your investigator to do. Begin by asking basic questions about the prospective investigator's qualifications and experience. If you think he sounds qualified, ask in a neutral way whether the investigator has worked for or knows of the group or person you are seeking information about—before disclosing precisely why you are interested. You may learn that he already knows something about the group because of a previous client or for some other reason. This could save you time and money. There is also a possibility that the prospective investigator will react enthusiastically, "Oh, I know a lot about The Searchers! My son goes to that church." It is not advisable to ask directly about any personal connection with a given group, but the investigator should disclose any potential conflicts of interest.

Next, if you want to continue the conversation, describe in general terms the information you need and ask the prospective investigator how he would go about getting it, how long it would take and what it would cost.

Query at least two prospective investigators as a check on the accuracy of their claims about the accessibility of the information and the cost of getting it. Costs may vary because of differences in rates or because one investigator has a more efficient way of getting the information you want. Most investigators charge an hourly fee, plus expenses. You can control costs by negotiating an agreement that authorizes a maximum charge. This means the investigator will keep track of his costs and will stop work before he exceeds the amount you've authorized.

In addition to information about an investigator's qualifications, experience, and methods of working, take note of his level of interest and enthusiasm about doing the job. Are your calls returned promptly? Do you get a follow-up call within a week or so to see if you've made your choice? Does the prospective investigator volunteer any additional ideas about getting information? If so, are they good ones?

Investigators are used to working with out-of-town clients and many have networks with other cities and areas of the country. If you know or can find a reputable investigator in your hometown, chances are good that he or she will be able to recommend someone in the place you are interested in. Other sources of names of private investigators might be attorneys, your employer and, of course, friends, family, and colleagues.

Once you've made your choice, it's a useful precaution to make the first project a specific, small, time-limited job, such as checking local property records for group property holdings. This way you will be able to judge if the investigator is doing a satisfactory job before you commit a large sum of money.

Finding a Thought Reform Consultant or Exit Counselor

You will probably have at most exactly one chance for an exit counseling intervention. It is therefore of the utmost importance to maximize your chances of success by choosing carefully the person or people who conduct the intervention. Thought reform consultants and exit counselors do not have a formal credentialing process and are not currently authenticated by any licensing board or other authority. Practitioners of this relatively new skill are still struggling to define themselves and evolve generally accepted principles and practices. A group of thought reform consultants have, as a first step, developed and subscribed to a Code of Ethics (available from AFF, American Family Foundation), and you might find it helpful to discuss this with prospective consultants during your talks with them.

Start your search for a thought reform consultant by reading *Exit Counseling; A Family Intervention*, by Carol Giambalvo, or by attending a presentation on exit counseling at a cult education conference. This will give you an idea of what exit counseling is and of the exit counselor's role.

At a minimum, a qualified thought reform consultant should have a thorough understanding of the elements of mind bending (or mind control, as most of them call it) and extensive experience in exit counseling. Knowledge of the group is important, but an experienced exit counselor can learn about the group as part of the preparation for the intervention. Exit counselors are usually former cult members. Most got their start in exit counseling by sitting in to help with interventions for members of their former groups.

The best way to select a thought reform consultant or exit counselor is to meet him or her in person and engage in long, serious conversation to determine how you get along and how he or she will come across to the cult member. It is essential to find someone whom you can trust and respect and whose perspective on cult involvement makes sense to you.

In addition to the usual information about background and experience, you will want to know about the prospective consultant's strategies and approaches, his ideas about your own case, what he would expect family members to do and what he would do. You want to know enough about this person that you can imagine him in conversation with your loved one and decide that he has the potential to engage her interest, and that at least there is nothing about him that will instantly turn her off.

The consultant need not be a model of beauty, but appearances are important. If the cult member is a fitness fanatic, you don't want her faced with an obese exit counselor. If the cult member has been taught that ministers of other sects are "of the devil" you may not want to start out with a consultant wearing a clerical collar, and so on.

Ask the prospective exit counselor about any history of involvement with the court system—lawsuits, arrests, and convictions, and if there is any, satisfy yourself that it is not relevant to your needs and will not affect an intervention.

Be cautious about anyone who claims that he has a "different" approach that is easier and doesn't require meticulous advance preparation or major input from the family. This may be true, but it isn't at this point known to mainstream cult researchers.

In addition to your personal impressions, try to find other families who have worked with the prospective consultant, especially, those whose intervention did not succeed. How do they feel about the experience and the exit counselor's role in it?

Finally, think about practical considerations—cost, ease of communication, flexibility on timing, and so forth. Will he or she be available if you can get the cult member to the place you have in mind? How will you handle unexpected scheduling changes? Is the prospective exit counselor accessible in case of emergency? Realistically, can you form with this particular person the partnership needed to maximize your chances of success?

The best sources for information about exit counselors or thought reform consultants are families and former members who have worked with them, particularly those who were involved in the same group as your family member. Try to find families that have engaged in both successful and unsuccessful interventions and ask who they retained and whether and why they would recommend that person to you. Families whose cult member is involved with large, well-known groups are likely to find qualified exit counselors experienced with the group and perhaps, formerly members of it. For those dealing with small groups, look for exit counselors experienced with similar groups, e.g., Bible-based, New Age, or self-improvement, for instance.

Attending a regional or national conference of a cult education organization is an excellent way to make contacts. These conferences attract former cult members, cult experts, and families with cult involvement problems. Airfare, hotel, and conference fees may seem costly, but this is an opportunity to meet many people who have helpful information and experiences to share, to speak with several prospective exit counselors, and to learn a great deal more about the cult phenomenon, all within a couple of days.

Finally, even the most careful selection can be an error. If, in the course of preparing for an intervention, you decide you have made a mistake, stop the process and look for someone else.

Appendix B
Information Resources

The Internet

The Internet is a fast, efficient way to a wealth of information about cults, about places and institutions, about local governments and, increasingly, information about specific groups, both pro and con. Information posted on the Internet is constantly being updated and you can get very recent and current reports.

The Internet is anarchical. There is practically no check or restraint on the information posted. It is easy and inexpensive to post information, misinformation, and disinformation. Abusive groups may lie about their structure, goals, and activities. Disgruntled individuals may lie about their experiences with certain groups. One group that has been the subject of many complaints is reported to be deliberately flooding the Internet with hundreds of Web sites touting their group, making it harder to find Web sites critical of the group. The word, "cult," lacking a clear definition, may be inaccurately (in this writer's opinion) applied to groups a person is angry about or used with an entirely different meaning, such as "fan club." There is no readily available formula for evaluating the accuracy or truthfulness of what you find on the Internet. Use it with caution.

If you do not have your own access to the Internet, check your local library or ask among your friends.

You can start your Internet investigation in several different ways:

- Search for information about the group by its name, or by its leader's name. Many groups have their own Web sites, which may offer valuable information about their ideology, history, and leadership.
- Go to www.culticstudies.org for AFF's (American Family Foundation's) Web site, copiously linked to sites dealing with information about cults and cultic groups;
- If the group has recently been in the news, look for news reports at major news sites like www.washingtonpost.com or www.nytimes.com.

- Consider asking AFF (American Family Foundation) to conduct a group search for you. AFF has at least a small amount of information on about 2000 groups, although there are probably thousands of others on which no information is available.

One site will lead you to the next and, if the group you are investigating is a large one, you may find that sorting and evaluating the mass of data is a bigger problem than getting it. Note the source of the information, the tone and perspective (or lack of perspective) of the presentation, the nature of the assertions made, and any evidence cited to back them up. Is the source likely to be biased? If so, in what respects? Is the posting angry and accusatory? Angry but rational? Sad? Over-enthusiastic? Coherent? Incoherent? As with any other encounter with a stranger—give it a chance, see what it says, but make your own appraisal.

Web Sites

General information

www.culticstudies.org (formerly known as www.csj.org)
> American Family Foundation home page. Links to sites on specific organizations (both pro and con), individuals' home pages, chat groups.

www.ex-cult.org/#cultlinks
> Ex-cult Archive, some specific groups listed

www.infocult.org
> Info-Cult/Secte - Canadian cult education organization

www.trancenet.org/
> trancenet.org Cult News Home Page

www.cesnur.org/
> Center for Studies in New Religions Home Page

www.yahoo.com/society_and_culture/religion/cults.
> Yahoo! - A well-organized index linked to a compendium of information covering specific groups, theory, history, etc.

Academic, theoretical orientation

www.americanreligion.org/index.html
> Institute for the Study of American Religion

cti.itc.virginia.edu/~jkh8x/soc257/cultsect/anticounter.htm
> New Religious Movements: Profiles

www.novareligio.com/
> Nova Religio - Journal of Alternative and Emergent Religions

www.religioustolerance.org/ocrt_hp/htm
Ontario Consultants on Religious Tolerance

Print Media

Books, magazines, scholarly journals, and newspapers are by no means superseded, especially for basic information that does not alter with time and classic works that pre-date the advent of the Internet. Books are also more convenient because you can carry them around with you, ready to read when and where you want. You don't have to have a computer or computer skills to "access" them and you need only a minimal investment to buy them. Unfortunately, many of the publications listed below are not readily available in public libraries, although some are. If you cannot find them in your library, many of them are available for purchase at cult education conferences or through cult education Web sites.

A. General information

AFF (American Family Foundation). *Cults and Psychological Abuse: A Resource Guide.* Bonita Springs, FL: AFF, 1999.

Cialdini, Robert B. *Influence: The New Psychology of Modern Persuasion.* New York: Quill, 1984.

Commission on Mental and Physical Disability Law, American Bar Association. *Cults in American Society: A Legal Analysis of Undue Influence, Fraud and Misrepresentation.* Washington, DC: CMPDL, 1995. (Reprinted in *Cultic Studies Journal,* Volume 12, Number 1, 1995.)

Enroth, Ronald M. *Churches That Abuse.* Grand Rapids, MI: Zondervan Publishing House, 1992.

Hassan, Steven. *Combating Cult Mind Control.* Rochester, VT: Park Street Press, 1988.

Hassan, Steven. *Releasing the Bonds.* Somerville, MA: Freedom of Mind Press, 2000.

Langone, Michael B. (Ed). *Recovery From Cults.* New York: W.W. Norton, 1993.

Ross, Joan Carol & Langone, Michael (Eds.). *Cults: What Parents Should Know.* New York: Carol Publishing Group, 1988.

Singer, Margaret T., & Lalich, Janja. *Cults in Our Midst: The Hidden Menace in Our Everyday Lives.* San Francisco: Jossey-Bass, 1995.

B. About Specific Groups

Atack, Jon. *A Piece of Blue Sky: Scientology, Dianetics and L. Ron Hubbard Exposed.* New York: Lyle Stuart, 1990.

Behar, Richard. "Scientology; The Cult of Greed," *Time Magazine*, May 6, 1991, pp. 32-39.

Butterfield, Stephen. *Amway: The Cult of Free Enterprise.* Boston: South End Press, 1985.

D'Antonio, Michael. "Fairfield, Iowa, Maharishi's Heaven on Earth," in *Heaven on Earth.* New York: Crown Publishers, 1992.

Giambalvo, Carol and Herbert Rosedale, Eds. *The Boston Movement: Critical Perspectives.* Bonita Springs, FL: American Family Foundation, 1996.

Hong, Nansook. *In the Shadow of the Moons.* Boston: Little, Brown and Co., 1998.

Kemperman, Steve. *Lord of the Second Advent.* Ventura, CA: Regal Books, 1984. (The author's experiences in the Unification Church)

Layton, Deborah. *Seductive Poison.* New York: Anchor Books, 1998 (The author's experiences in the People's Temple).

Laxer, Mark. *Take Me for a Ride: Coming of Age in a Destructive Cult.* College Park, MD: Outer Rim Press, 1993. (The author's experiences in "Rama," led by Frederick Lenz)

McWilliams, Peter. *Life 102; What to Do When Your Guru Sues You.* (John-Roger and MSIAH) Los Angeles: Prelude Press, 1994.

Persinger, Michael, Normand J. Carrey and Lynn A. Suess. *TM and Cult Mania.* North Quincy, MA: The Christopher Publishing House, 1980.

Pressman, Steven. *Outrageous Betrayal; The Dark Journey of Werner Erhard from est to Exile.* New York: St. Martin's Press, 1993.

Reed, David A. *How to Rescue Your Loved One from the Watchtower.* Grand Rapids, MI: Baker Book House, 1989.

Underwood, Barbara & Betty. *Hostage to Heaven.* New York: Clarkson N. Potter, Inc., 1979. (Out of print). (Unification Church)

C. How-to Books

Giambalvo, Carol. *Exit Counseling; A Family Intervention.* Bonita Springs, FL: American Family Foundation, 1992.

Gunderson, Ted L. *How to Locate Anyone Anywhere.* New York: Penguin Group, 1991.

Tillman, Norma Mott. *How to Find Almost Anyone, Anywhere.* Nashville, TN: Rutledge Hill Press, 1994.

Zilliox, Jr., Larry & Kahaner, Larry. *How to Investigate Destructive Cults and Underground Groups.* Alexandria, VA: KANE Associates International, Inc., 1990.

Recovery

Ford, Wendy. *Recovery from Abusive Groups.* Bonita Springs, FL: American Family Foundation, 1993.

Tobias, Madeleine & Lalich, Janja. *Captive Heart Captive Minds; Freedom and Recovery from Cults and Abusive Relationships.* Alameda, CA: Hunter House, 1994.

Caution regarding "Cult Awareness Network"(CAN)

On October 23, 1996, a law firm which represented the Church of Scientology for years purchased the logo and license agreement of the Cult Awareness Network (CAN). Accordingly, any publications or communications using the CAN name or logo after October 23, 1996 should not be regarded as emanating from or having the approval of the Cult Awareness Network personnel or officers who were associated with CAN before 23 October 1996.

Several older publications refer you to the "Cult Awareness Network" (CAN) in Illinois. That phone line and address are no longer trustworthy. The Illinois phone number and a very similar address were acquired by Scientology-related investors in California, who also set up a similarly named Web site. The new "CAN" operators assert that mind control does not exist, contrary to the position of the original CAN, yet claim that they are the oldest cult information group in the country, as if they were the original CAN. It has been asserted that they have even reported a mother's concern about a group to the group in question. Despite a complaint that the new "CAN" management makes deceptive use of the "CAN" name, the Attorney General of California has failed to act.